PCD ASSOCIATES – *Books*

ARCHITECTS, CONSULTANTS AND PROJECT MANAGERS

THE
CREATIVE
ENTREPRENEURS

unlocking entrepreneurial potentials

by
Arc. M.B. Bello, fnia
Principal Architect
Founder of PCD Associates since May 22nd 1990

www. pcdassociates. com

Published by Dolman Scott in 2018

ISBNs
Book: 978-1-911412-79-3
iBooks: 978-1-911412-80-9
Kindle: 978-1-911412-81-6

Dolman Scott Ltd
www.dolmanscott.co.uk

Gi - 01

"Limitless entrepreneurial opportunities are opened to those who consistently think of value creation"

———

Author

———

CONTENTS

Acknowledgements

This is to acknowledge and thank all who contributed immensely to the success of this book. I first of all would like to thank my wife, Farida Bello, for her diligent search for references that added value to this book. She also researched and gave content to chapters eight and nine of the book. Muhammed Bello, Shittu Shamsudeen, Faith Fatunwase, I thank you for your assiduous research on topics that contributed to several chapters of this book. Olamide Eso, who designed the book cover and added illustrations, fine-tuned the content and sequence of the book in preparation for final publishing. Also acknowledged are Mansur Bello and Kayode Karunwi for their expert advice regarding the final look of the illustrations. Munir Bello is also acknowledged for identifying a most reputable publisher. Jerry Ugwu was of immense help in the critique of the first manuscript of this book. Finally, I would like to express my gratitude to Enesi Makoju, who agreed to write the Foreword. His write-up captures the very essence of the book. Also, Aliu Akoshile's succinct summary provided the synopsis of the book. This book would not have been a reality without you all. I am immensely grateful for all your support. Thank you.

Arc. M.B. Bello, fnia

Foreword

There are four key factors of production, namely: land, labour, capital and entrepreneurship.

Entrepreneurship is typically regarded as the most critical of all these factors as it is the process of organising and optimising the utilisation of all the other factors of production to create value and, of course, profit therein. In the course of my twenty-three years of post-graduate work experience, I had the unique privilege of working as a venture-capital fund manager for eleven years in a leading bank. My functions were largely established around making equity investments and managing these investments on behalf of the bank in an array of small and medium-sized enterprises across various sectors of the Nigerian economy. I was directly involved in evaluating hundreds of Small Medium Enterprises (SMEs) seeking investment, and ended up directly participating in the management of over fifty SMEs, where the bank eventually invested its funds as equity.

This unique experience enabled me to engage directly with many entrepreneurs, with intensive relationships established with over fifty promoters of businesses in the day-to-day management of their companies towards achieving their objectives of profit and growth.

In the process of dealing and relating with these entrepreneurs, I have come to the realisation that there are certain characteristics and traits that are extremely common amongst the successful entrepreneurs.

Successful entrepreneurs, in my opinion, are those entrepreneurs who have the unique ability to organise all other factors of production plus time in the most optimal manner, such that they are able to achieve sustainable value for all stakeholders relevant to their businesses, i.e. shareholders, staff, financiers, suppliers, customers, government, etc.

Successful entrepreneurship is not just about being able to significantly generate profit and growth in the short term, but is more about being able to provide consistent value for stakeholders over the long term. I have observed that the entrepreneurs who were able to achieve this exhibited the following traits and characteristics:

1   **Overcoming the "Agency Dilemma"** – Successful entrepreneurs are able to distinguish between their own personal needs and the needs of the enterprise, and understand that in the management of the enterprise's resources, priority must be given to the enterprise's needs over their personal needs.

2   **Creativity and Innovation** – Successful entrepreneurs have a passion for achieving differentiation in both their products and their processes. They are never satisfied with doing things the way others are doing them. They constantly seek out more efficient processes towards producing more effective products.

3   **Focus on Numbers and Records** – Successful entrepreneurs understand the benefits that come with setting up robust management information systems (MIS). They keep details of all transactions and constantly analyse historical data towards effectively projecting for the future.

4   **Leveraging Technology** – The modern-day successful entrepreneur is very up to date with technological development and is very adept at applying technology in leveraging his organisation's value chain.

5   **Prudence and Financial Responsibility** – The successful entrepreneur is very cautious about taking on loans and other forms of interest-bearing finance just for the sake of it. They are wary of exposing themselves to debt and will only draw down on such when absolutely necessary.

6   **Mindful of the Competition** – Successful entrepreneurs are sometimes obsessed with the activities of their competitors, not wanting to lose market share in anyway.

7   **Obsessed with their Customers** – Successful entrepreneurs are those who have reached the peak in the hierarchy of the customer retention/expansion pyramid. They have moved from the placid idea of customer service, or customer loyalty, to the realm of customer obsession. Successful entrepreneurs characteristically tailor their products/services towards solving current, and more importantly, anticipated needs of their actual and potential customers based on data-driven feedback processes.

8   Sensitive to the Needs of Employees – Successful entrepreneurs do not take their employees for granted. They want to train and retain the best in the market and are good at managing and leading their employees.

9   "The Value of Relationships" – Perhaps what I have come to observe as the most distinguishing features of successful entrepreneurs is their unique ability to "leverage relationships in the creation of value". For many successful entrepreneurs, relationships can be a more impactful factor of production than cash/capital. They are able to establish, maintain and grow relationships with individuals and organisations that are strategic to their business and discretely exploit these relationships in harnessing market opportunities.

It is in view of all the above that the author of this book, Arc. M.B. Bello, who himself is a very successful entrepreneur, has chosen to share information valuable and useful to aspiring entrepreneurs who seek to attain sustainable success in their chosen endeavours. I find the content of this book, which is quite extensive in its breadth of content, a very useful tool, as it validates a lot of my first-hand observations in the course of my career.

Enjoy and learn while you read.

Enesi Makoju
Venture-Capital Fund Manager

*"You can't use up creativity; the more you use,
the more you have"*

———————

Maya Angelou

———————

Dedication

This book is dedicated to

all entrepreneurs and aspiring entrepreneurs in

the Creative Industry

who continously use their creativity

for wealth creation in the economies of

nations across the world.

Gi - 03

"Every creative entrepreneur must fill a void or address a specific economic opportunity"

———

Adetu Seni

———

INTRODUCTION

The creative industries – unlocking entrepreneurial potentials

The economy of a nation and indeed the world is largely dependent on the activities of the creative industries.

The world has now understood how the likes of Bill Gates, Mark Zukerberg, etc, have transformed how we perceive, communicate and do things. Certainly, without the Information Technology in today's world, your guess is as good as mine.

Accordingly, this book seeks to provide the appropriate super-highway guide by a creative Architect Entrepreneur on the relevance and corresponding deployment of creative assets of individuals and groups following their uplift as entrepreneurs/investors into the building of a vibrant and viable economy through the creation of jobs and wealth on a sustainable basis.

The book is useful for would-be creative entrepreneurs, investors, as well as policy-makers who need to understand the workings of the creative industries.

The difference between entrepreneurship and investment, as well as their correlation with the economy, will be clearly illustrated in subsequent chapters.

It is hoped that the reader will benefit from the immense wealth of experience of the creative Architect Entrepreneur as a viable guide for all the aspiring creative entrepreneurs/investors in the deployment of their intellectual property (IP) assets for growing their businesses for profit and sustainability. The respective nation will be the better for it, as the economy is expected to witness a continually sustained growth.

This book has identified and defined all the various professions that form the nucleus of the creative industries. The book has made very strong attempts to link the various professions together and indeed the inter-relationship for mutual benefit.

Entrepreneurship understanding and ability is the vehicle required to take the individual creative asset to the marketplace. An excellent knowledge of entrepreneurship translates into a success, directly or indirectly.

The Economy:

THE ECONOMY OF creativity

Gi - 04

A given economy is the outcome of contextual factors that shape the condition and determine the parameters with which it functions and is influenced by a set of processes that include its culture, values, education, technological evolution, history, social practices, political structure and legal systems, as well as natural endowment and ecology.

However, an economy can witness a boom or recession. But for all times' sake, a balanced economy will generally be sufficient for the comfort of a nation.

The entrepreneurs and investors are certainly amongst the most important players within a given economy, as jobs have to be created before wealth can be realised. So it means entrepreneurs have to be made with a view to encouraging investors to be interested in the economy.

The creative entrepreneurs will always remain at the centre of a healthy economic development, as it is with the state of California – the creative entrepreneurial investors' haven of the United States of

America. The subsequent chapters will show how to grow the right set of creative entrepreneurs. The movie industries will effectively tell our own stories, whilst our architects can develop the right concept in real-time space management, as this will reach the marketplace through the best advertisement presentation model and modus.

The story will never be the same again, as we will begin to experience very dynamic desired economic growth on a continually sustained basis for transformation like never before.

Successful creative entrepreneurs are the effective engine room of the nation's economy. The whole economy will be transformed as soon as the potentials of the creative persons have been effectively unlocked. This was the strategy adopted by most of the States of America. The book also gives guidance on setting up finance, accounting and taxation matters, along with providing the right guidelines on how to attract investors to your enterprises.

Finally, the book gives a guideline on how to create your own strategy for making successful enterprises without compromising your creative assets, as well as being futuristic in nature for sustainability as a panacea to avoiding pitfalls that may arise from trading your intellectual assets.

The content of this book has been well articulated by a creative Architect Entrepreneur with over 30 years of proven experience and track record.

I trust you will find the entire content useful as either a pleasure, business development, or, indeed, an appropriate guide to unlocking your innate potentials for your own good and the transformation of our economy and other economies.

Thank you.

1 The Creative Industries

CREATIVE
INDUSTRIES

Gi – 05a   Gi – 05b

*"Audacious ambition with spectacular execution can create
respectable return on investors' fund"*

Foreshore Waters

THE CREATIVE INDUSTRIES

Creativity can be viewed as an innate expression of intrinsic energy, cognitive ability and related characteristics of an individual in response to the perception of needful communication and provision of solutions to a perceived need in a particular environment with or without limit. Thus leads to outward exhibition of processed ideas in diverse forms with economic and entrepreneurial potentials.

The creative industries refer to a range of economic activities which are concerned with the generalisation or exploitation for knowledge and information.

Gi - 06

The socio-economic potential of the creative industries activities have now been fully recognised by governments and investors across the world for its importance as a generator of jobs, wealth and cultural engagements. They are capable of forming the nucleus for a more pragmatic social cohesion, re-orientation and sustainable economic development of a nation.

Creative entrepreneurial activities stand unified by the use of intellectual property (IP) to protect the trade in creative assets, for proper realisation of economic value by creative entrepreneurs. It is strongly perceived as a common factor and most deserving of topmost attention.

A creative person may not necessarily be an entrepreneur. The content of this book is to create the right understanding and developmental guide for the creative person to become a successful entrepreneur. The approach is to bring to bear all the necessary requirements and understanding for the creative person. As the products and services of the creative person have to be traded in the market place, this approach cannot be undermined. Accordingly, with more creative persons embracing entrepreneurial training skills, we can begin to see the effect of the creative industries by the unlocking of all the potentials for the economic transformation that lies therein.

This book provides a complete understanding of just how to realise these facts.

The content of this book focuses on Nigeria as a model and may indeed be applicable anywhere else globally.

It does not preclude academic interest though originating from a well-tested and proven creative architect entrepreneur who had deployed his intellectual property asset to set the stage right for common good.

* * *

The creative industries listings

Gi – 07

"Those industries that are based on individual creativity, skill and talent, with the potential to create wealth and jobs through developing intellectual property, include thirteen sectors:

1. Advertising
2. Architecture
3. Art and the Antique Market
4. Crafts
5. Design
6. Designer Fashion
7. Film
8. Interactive Leisure – Software (video games, etc.)
9. Music
10. Performing Arts
11. Publishing
12. Software
13. Television and radio"

An understanding of the workings of these industries will provide the key to unlocking the potential that exists therein.

The sectors can be further grouped as follows in recognition of their interrelationships;

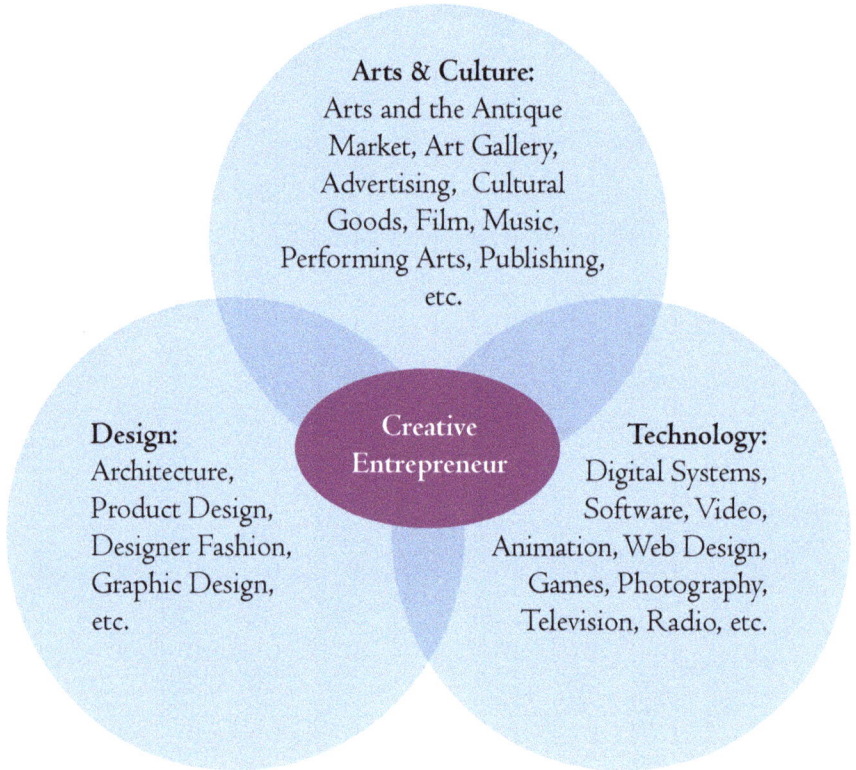

Arts & Culture:
Arts and the Antique Market, Art Gallery, Advertising, Cultural Goods, Film, Music, Performing Arts, Publishing, etc.

Design:
Architecture, Product Design, Designer Fashion, Graphic Design, etc.

Creative Entrepreneur

Technology:
Digital Systems, Software, Video, Animation, Web Design, Games, Photography, Television, Radio, etc.

Ci – 08

The overlapping nature of the creative industries and their sectors

1. Advertising

Gi – 09

To attract realistic demand for goods or services especially in a competitive environment, creative entrepreneurs advertise their offerings using the right combination of media.

Advertising is defined as "an audio or visual form of marketing communication that employs an openly sponsored, non-personal message to promote or sell a product, service or idea." Advertising is sponsored by businesses to promote their products i.e. goods or services. It is paid for and the advertiser has control over the full message, this differentiates it from public relations. Similarly, message in advertising is usually directed to target consumer groups of the public or the larger public and not to a particular individual, which therefore differentiates it from personal selling.

Advertising is communicated through various mass media,[7] including old media such as newspapers, magazines, television, radio, outdoor advertising or direct mail, and online news media such as search results, blogs, websites or text messages, such as WhatsApp. The actual message is presented as an advertisement simply referred to as 'ad'. Increasing consumer size and demand is the main aim of commercial ads especially to generate brand loyalty for their products or services through brand name or image associated with perceived good qualities by the consumers. Direct response advertising use ads that intend to generate immediate sale.

–   Companies use their brands to depict quality and association with product name and image, and subsequently in commercial ads to attract increased demand.

–   Also direct response advertising is a high-impact and short-term response generator. It is deployed to generate instant sales and most suitable for consumer goods, communication and other services, events registration, and so on.

–   Non-commercial advertising is commonly used by non-profit oriented organisations such as religious organisations, social groups, political parties, pressure groups like employment and other unions, non-government organisations and governmental agencies.

A public service announcement may be used as free mode of persuasion. Similarly, it was suggested that employees or shareholders may be targeted by this mode of advertising to reassure them of the viability or success of a company. An example is when advertising is used as a vehicle for cultural assimilation, encouraging workers to exchange their traditional habits and community structure in favour of shared modern life for societal re-orientation for growth.

Generally, projection for advertisement in the media in 2017 spread as follows:

40.4% on TV, 33.3% on digital, 9% on newspapers, 6.9% on magazines, 5.8% on outdoor and 4.3% on radio. In 2015 also, the estimated media spend globally on advertisements is big business, with an estimated projected spend for 2015 reservedly at US$592.43 billion.

Accordingly, advertising has been transformed: from dates back to using papyrus in 4000BC, then through newsprints in the 19th Century, followed by the 20th century, when the trending was from radio in the 1920s, television in the 1950s, cable television in the 1980s, the internet from the 1990s, to the diverse media including online and mobile apps and still transforming. It was used as a major campaign for selling products by Thomas J Barratt: "Good morning. Have you used Pears Soap?" – a famous advert of the 20th century.

Classification:

There are different ways by which advertising is categorised, including by style, medium, purpose, geographic scope or target audience.

–   Ads in print advertising classified by style can include display advertising (ads with design elements sold by size).

- Classified advertising, especially in print – ads without design elements sold by word or line, commonly placed in newspaper.

- Global, national or local advertising that limits or delimits the spread of the ad.

- Brand advertising is usually to raise awareness as the main purpose.

- Direct response advertising is used to generate immediate sale.

Depending on the nature of the business and the target customer and consumer, be it business to business (B2B) or business to consumer (B2C), this informs whether the ad campaign be directed to target businesses or consumers directly.

The new trend in advertising

Nowadays, media broadcasting follows a new trend whereby the internet is the favourite for news and music, while the use of digital video recorders (DVR) and similar devices is the practice.

Online communication channels now provide a more convenient advertising media, with almost direct access to the marketplace.

It is all about awareness. The future trend will include niche markets, crowd sourcing, global advertising, foreign public messaging, diversification, new technology, advertising for education purposes, sales promotions and brand loyalty.

Finally, I will limit this to the understating of ads. It will, however, be necessary for government to regulate practices to protect her citizens within a geographical location. There are also institutions and associations of practitioners; this will include the World Federation of Advertisers responsible for harmonisation of quality of practice.

2. Architecture

Gi – 11

"Architecture" means: 'The art and science in theory and practice of design, erection, commissioning, maintenance and management and co- ordination of allied professional inputs thereto of buildings, or part thereof, and layout and master plan of such buildings or groups of buildings forming a comprehensive institution, establishment or neighbourhood, as well as any other organised space, enclosed or open, required for human and other activities.'

Architecture and Practice

Architecture

Here's what the American Architect Frank Lloyd Wright wrote about Architecture:

"What is Architecture anyway? Is it the vast collection of various buildings which have been built to please the varying taste of the various lords of mankind? I think not.

"No, I know that architecture is life; or at least it is life itself taking form and therefore it is the truest record of life as it was lived in the world yesterday, as it is lived today or ever will be lived. So architecture I know to be a Great Spirit... Architecture is that great living creative spirit which from generation to generation, from age to age, proceeds, persists, creates, according to the nature of man, and his circumstances as they change. That is really architecture" Frank Lloyd Wright, from *In The Realm of Ideas.*

The Architect

The Architect (*pronounced as ahr — ki — tekt*) is a person who engages in the profession of architecture.

"**Architect**" means any person professionally entitled to registration under the Architects Registration Council of Nigeria (ARCON) Act of 1990 Cap 20 Laws of the Federation of Nigeria; who is authorised to practise Architecture.

Architecture and Practice

Professional practice involves the "use of one's knowledge in a particular profession"; besides, professional practice is prevalent in the field of architecture, law, biomedicine related to health care, engineering, medicine, accounting, etc. Architecture is the only discipline which encompasses the four major fields of human endeavour: humanities, arts, science and technology.

Every creative entrepreneur must endeavuor to associate with relevant professional body which is entrusted to regulate the practice as well as to organise activities and training events that offer networking and synergy among people of same and related professions.

3.   Arts and the Antique Market

Art market – a physical or figurative venue where works of arts are brought, displayed, bought and sold. Here collectible objects of different products, years and sources are available for direct sale or purchase and often through an agent who represents the principal seller or buyer. The common definition of antique is "a collectible object such as a piece of furniture or work of art that has a high value because of its considerable age." The source, product, and year are very significant and influence the value attributed to the collectible object.

Similarly, the antique market offers collectible objects considered to be of high value due to the retention of its quality and original condition over a period not less than 100years. "In the United States, the 1930 Smoot-Hawley Tariff Act defined antiques as... works of art (except rugs and carpets made after the year 1700), collections in illustration of the progress of the arts, works in bronze, marble, terracotta, parian, pottery, or porcelain, artistic antiquities and objects of ornamental character or educational value which shall have been produced prior to the year 1830. Motor vehicles are an exception to the 100-year rule. Also, anything old with class by Wayne Mattox was further extended with anything that gives you happiness; in other words, anything old with class that brings you happiness.

On the other hand, antiquities a close term, refers to things of the past such as remains of ancient art and everyday items which are also considered archaeological artefacts. A person who collects and studies antiquities or things of the past is referred to as an antiquarian.

4. Crafts

A profession or pastime in skilled work with specific skills and knowledge is referred to as craft or trade. In the past, people occupied in small-scale production of goods, or their maintenance were of this category and in high demand. They are the artisans of diverse vocations today which replaced the terms 'craftsman' and 'craftswoman' of the past.

Usually, there are more craftsmen in urban centres than the suburb areas due to the difference in economic value both locations offer. They are found in guilds of specific trades where they disseminate information, train, develop as well as derive professional confidence among others. They often engage in continuous skills training and development to improve their capability towards meeting current realities. Nowadays, artisans i.e. people in trades and crafts are of better economic balance than those of the past who had to rely on exchange of goods with people in agricultural works to meet their household needs.

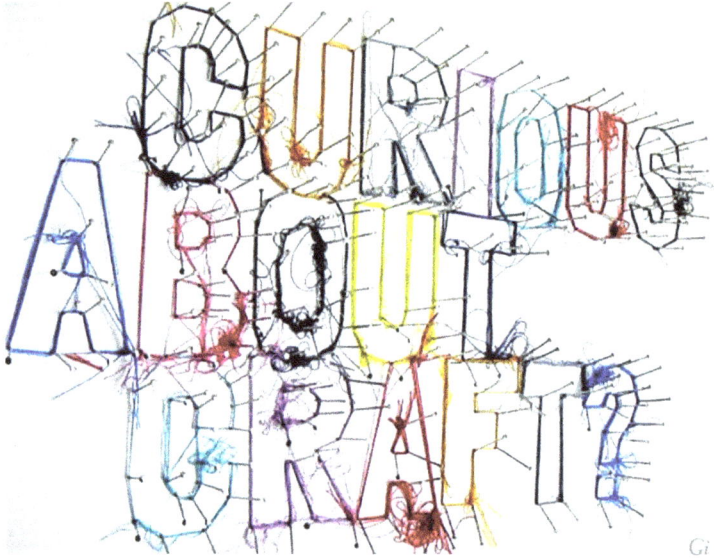

Gi – 13

The making of a craft or trade person starts from being an apprentice under the tutelage and guidance of a master of the craft. On completion of the apprenticeship the apprentice becomes a journeyman. At this stage most will set up a shop to make a living from there and subsequently master the craft and be considered a master of the craft. This format of training and progression still continues today in many parts of the world, Nigeria is an example, though the crafts sector has experienced significant changes since during the industrial revolution.

Although the mass production of goods by large-scale industry has strong effect on the demand for crafts, craftspeople still find demand from niche market segments that are not satisfied by mass-produced goods. They are able to adapt semi-finished components or materials from the industries in their crafts to meet customers' requirements or demands, thereby engage in deliberate collaboration with the industry.

5. Design

"Design is the creation of a plan or convention for the construction of an object, system or measurable human interaction". This is so in architectural blueprints, engineering drawings, business processes, circuit diagrams, and sewing patterns. Design has different connotations in different fields. In some cases, the direct construction of an object (as in pottery, engineering, management, coding, and graphic design) is also considered to use design thinking.

Designing often necessitates considering the aesthetic, functional, economic and socio-political dimensions of both the design object and design process. It may involve considerable research, thought, modelling, interactive adjustment, and re-design. Meanwhile, diverse kinds of objects may be designed, including clothing, graphical user interfaces, skyscrapers, corporate identities, business processes, and even methods or processes of designing."

6. Designer Fashion

Fashion design is the art of application of design and aesthetics or natural beauty to clothing and accessories. Fashion design is influenced by cultural and social attitudes, and has varied over time and place. Fashion designers work in a number of ways in designing clothing and accessories such as bracelets and necklaces. Because of the time required to bring a garment onto the market, designers must at times anticipate changes to consumer tastes.

Gi – 16

Designers conduct research on fashion trends and interpret them for their audience. Their specific designs are used by manufacturers. This is the essence of a designer's role; however, there is variation within this that is determined by the buying and merchandising approach, and product quality; for example, budget retailers will use inexpensive fabrics to interpret trends, but high-end retailers will ensure that the best available fabrics are used.

7. Film

Gi – 17

Film, also called a movie, motion picture, theatrical film, or photoplay, is a series of still images that when shown on a screen, create an illusion of motion images (due to the phi phenomenon).

This optical illusion causes the audience to perceive continuous motion between separate objects viewed rapidly in succession. The process of film-making is both an art and an industry. A film is created by photographing actual scenes with a motion-picture camera; by photographing drawings or miniature models using traditional animation techniques, by means of computer generated images (CGI) and computer animation; or by a combination of some or all of these techniques and other visual effects.

8. Interactive Leisure Software (video games, etc.)

Digital content and applications produced by the creative industries include the output of the computer games industry, websites, digital video arts and digital film and television production covering text, graphics, special effects, animation and post-production. Digital content and applications are also produced in the fields of news media, music, architecture and design, and education and health.

The Interactive Leisure Software industry over the last thirty years has moved from a cottage industry to one dominated by publicly owned global publishers.

The industry is divided into: Console (video games), devices plugged into television and are played using joypads; and PC (computer games). It is open as to which is of general benefit.

The leisure software now surpasses the gross revenue of cinema admission or video rental in a lot of developed countries. The video games market is now worth over US $15 billion. The USA, Japan and the UK are the world leaders in terms of consumption.

One of the key studies is the PricewaterhouseCoopers Entertainment and Media Outlook, which provides global analyses and market forecasts for 14 industry segments, including television networks (broadcast and cable) and distribution (station, cable, and satellite), filmed entertainment, recorded music, video games, radio, books, newspapers and magazine publishing, as well as advertising, theme and amusement parks, and sports. It estimates that the global trade was worth $1.2 trillion in 2003 and rose to $2.2 trillion in 2012.

The PWC 2008 report also indicates that as a share of the global creative economy, digital and mobile distribution rose from 5% in 2007 to 11% in 2012, the equivalent of $234 billion. The data presented for 2007 shows that the recorded music industry is the front-runner, with digital revenues accounting for 15% of the industry. The interactive leisure software industry is now dominated by publicity owned global publishers selling to mass market. Publishers pay no fees and seek no permission to make PC games. Popular PC games include:

- Nintendo Wii
- 8 Wonders of the World
- Tomb Raider
- Ghost Master

The game industry is technology driven and depends on the continued introduction of faster, more graphically sophisticated hardware. It is an inherently dynamic industry subject to technology and product life-cycles of limited duration. Online gaming in virtual worlds is far more than a new form of entertainment; it is also a new kind of cultural form, from which is emerging real creativity, real economic value and real relationships.

Editors at *Game Developer* magazine, the leading video game industry publication, in the USA, released the results of its eighth annual *Game Developer* Salary Survey (2009), calculating an average American game industry salary in 2008 of $79,000, a 7% increase from 2007's figure of nearly $74,000.

Programming: programmers are the highest paid talent next to high-end businesspeople, with an average annual salary of $85,024. Experience pays in this role, as those with greater than six years of experience earned 26% more than the average annual salary.

Art & Animation: Artists average a $69,532 salary; nonetheless, 28% of art directors reported lower salaries than the previous year. But these more experienced, higher-status artists also tend to earn at least 35% more than those with less experience and lower title.

Game Design: Averaging $67,379, design positions sprouted an average $3,730 over the previous year. As with many roles, region makes a difference, given that West Coast designers make on average $8,283 or 12% more than the rest of the game designers in the country.

9. Music

Gi – 18

An art of sound in time that expresses ideas and emotions in significant forms through the elements of rhythm, melody, harmony, and colour;

the tones or sounds employed, occurring in single line (melody) or multiple lines (harmony), and sounded or to be sounded by one or more voices or instruments, or both compositions for singing or playing.

10. Performing Arts

Performing arts are forms of art in which artists use their voices or bodies, often in relation to other objects, to convey artistic expression. It is different from visual arts, which is when artists use paint, canvas or various materials to create physical or static art objects. Performing arts include several disciplines, each performed in front of a live audience.

Theatre, music, dance, and other kinds of performances are present in all human cultures. The history of music and dance dates to pre-historic times. More refined versions, such as ballet, opera, and Kabuki, are performed professionally.

Live performance before an audience is a form of entertainment. The development of audio and video recording has allowed for private consumption of the performing arts.

The performing arts can help explain our emotions, expressions, and feelings. Artists who participate in performing arts in front of an audience are called performers. Examples of these include actors, comedians, dancers, magicians, circus artistes, musicians, and singers. Performing arts are also supported by workers in related fields, such as song-writing, choreography and stagecraft.

A performer who excels in acting, singing, and dancing is commonly referred to as a triple threat. Well-known examples of historical triple threat artists include Gene Kelly, Fred Astaire, and Judy Garland.

Performers often adapt their appearance, such as with costumes and stage make-up, stage lighting, and sound.

11. Publishing

Publishing is the dissemination of literature, music, or information – the activity of making information available to the general public. In some cases, authors may be their own publishers, meaning originators and developers of content also provide media to deliver and display the content for the same. Also, the word publisher can refer to the individual who leads a publishing company or an imprint or to a person who owns/heads a magazine.

Traditionally, the term refers to the distribution of printed works such as books (the "book trade") and newspapers. With the advent of digital information systems and the Internet, the scope of publishing has expanded to include electronic resources such as the electronic versions of books and periodicals, as well as micropublishing, websites, blogs, video game publishers, and the like.

Publishing includes the following stages of development: acquisition, copy editing, production, printing (and its electronic equivalents), and marketing and distribution.

Gi — 20

Publication is also important as a legal concept:

As the process of giving formal notice to the world of a significant intention; for example, to marry or enter bankruptcy;

As the essential precondition of being able to claim defamation; that is, the alleged libel must have been published, and

For copyright purposes, where there is a difference in the protection of published and unpublished works.

There are two categories of book publisher:

i. Non-paid publishers: A non-paid publisher is a publication house that does not charge authors at all to publish their books. They command certain rights to publish the work and pay royalty on books sold. This is traditional publisher also known as commercial publisher.

ii. Paid publishers: The author has to meet with the total expense to get the book published, and the author has full right to set up marketing policies. This is self-publishing, also known as vanity publishing.

12. Software

Software is a general term for the various kinds of programs used to operate computers and related devices. (The term 'hardware' describes the physical aspects of computers and related devices.)

Software can be thought of as the variable part of a computer and hardware the invariable part. Software is often divided into application software (programs that do work users are directly interested in) and system software (which includes operating systems and any program that supports application software). The term middleware is sometimes used to describe programming that mediates between application and system software or between two different kinds of application software (for example, sending a remote work request from an application in a computer that has one kind of operating system to an application in a computer with a different operating system).

An additional and difficult-to-classify category of software is the utility, which is a small, useful program with limited capability. Some utilities come with operating systems. Like applications, utilities tend to be separately installable and capable of being used independently from the rest of the operating system.

Applets are small applications that sometimes come with the operating system as 'accessories'. They can also be created independently using Java or other programming languages.

Software can be purchased or acquired as shareware (usually intended for sale after a trial period), liteware (shareware with some capabilities disabled), freeware (free software, but with copyright restrictions), public domain software (free with no restrictions), and open source (software where the source code is furnished and users agree not to limit the distribution of improvements).

Software is often packaged on CD-ROMs and diskettes. Today, much purchased software, shareware, and freeware is downloaded over the Internet. A new trend is software that is made available for use at another site known as an application service provider.

Some general kinds of application software include:

iii.   Productivity software, which includes word processors, spreadsheets, and tools for use by most computer users

iv.   Presentation software

v.   Graphics software for graphic designers

vi.   CAD/CAM software

vii.   Specialised scientific applications

viii.   Vertical market or industry-specific software (for example, for banking, insurance, retail, and manufacturing environments).

13. Television and Radio

Gi – 21

Transmission of radio and television programmes from a radio or television station to home receivers by radio waves is referred to as "over the air" (OTA) or terrestrial broadcasting, and in most countries it requires a broadcasting licence. Transmissions using a wire or cable, like cable television (which also retransmits OTA stations with their consent), are also considered broadcasts, but do not necessarily require a licence (though in some countries a licence is required). In the 2000s, transmissions of television and radio programmes via streaming digital technology have increasingly been referred to as broadcasting as well. A broadcast may be distributed through several physical means. If coming directly from the radio studio at a single station or television station, it is simply sent through the studio/transmitter link to the transmitter and whence from the television antenna located on the radio masts and towers out to the world.

Programming may also come through a communications satellite, played either live or recorded for later transmission. Networks of stations may simulcast the same programming at the same time, originally via microwave link, now usually by satellite. Distribution to stations or networks may also be through physical media, such as magnetic tape, compact disc (CD), DVD, and sometimes other formats. Usually, these are included in another broadcast, such as when electronic news-gathering (ENG) returns a story to the station for inclusion on a news programme.

2 Entrepreneurship, Entrepreneur and Enterprise

Gi – 23

"Turn your passion into a life-long successful commercial adventure, Be real! Be Happy!"

Anonymous

ENTREPRENEURSHIP, ENTREPRENEUR AND ENTERPRISE

Entrepreneurship

Entrepreneurship is the capacity and willingness to develop, organise and manage a business venture along with any accompanying risks in order to make a profit.

Entrepreneurship depicts job creation and management in a profitable manner as a result of identified business opportunity in a business environment. The creativity and wealth generation in entrepreneurship usually add value to a nation's wealth and development in aggregate nature from different sectors of the economy. Innovation, risk-taking, business development and sound organisation are some of the skills that entrepreneurship demands.

The most obvious example of entrepreneurship is the starting up of a new business.

Many schools of thought agree that entrepreneurship is characterised by creativity, innovation and the initiative to set-up and nurture a business venture. Entrepreneurship contributes to nation's economic success and its ability to compete favourably in the current dynamic global marketplace.

In entrepreneurship, there are two sides of the coin, especially in the introductory period of the business and the early years. The business may turnover profitably or at an unexpected loss. The understanding of how business works, through learning, and the performance and resilience of other similar businesses, coupled with own passion and desire to succeed will offer succour to forge on towards better future performance.

6+6 Drivers for Entrepreneurship

Growth, Achievement	Humanity, Spirituality
• To follow a passion	• To pursue a mission
• To pursue a vision	• To create new value
• To create and innovate	• To help people
• To seize opportunities	• To improve the World
• To find excitement	• To facilitate growth
• To create wealth	• To spread spiritually

Gi – 24

● ● ●

Entrepreneur

A person, who exercises initiative by organising a venture to take advantage of an opportunity, and as a decision-maker, decides what and how much of good or service needs to be produced by managing and assuming the risks of a business or enterprise.

A significant proportion of new businesses fail due to either high risk in launching a start-up, insufficient funding, an economic crisis, lack of market demand or bad business decisions. However, with the proper tools and research, aspiring entrepreneurs can become successful when a good strategy and goals are set in place prior to starting a project and eventually satisfying the desired outcome and objectives of a business venture.

The entrepreneur is often an innovator with new ideas developed into business activities. Essentially, leadership attributes, management skills and strong team-building abilities are desirable for optimal success.

There are different types of entrepreneurs, one or more of which each entrepreneur can identify with according to Clarence Danhof (1949) classification and that of other behavioural Scientists.

Types of Entrepreneurs

1. Business-type Entrepreneurs
2. Technology-type Entrepreneurs
3. Ownership-based Entrepreneurs
4. Gender-based Entrepreneurs
5. Size-based Entrepreneurs
6. Circumstantial Entrepreneurs
7. Behavioural-based Entrepreneurs

THE ENTREPRENEUR

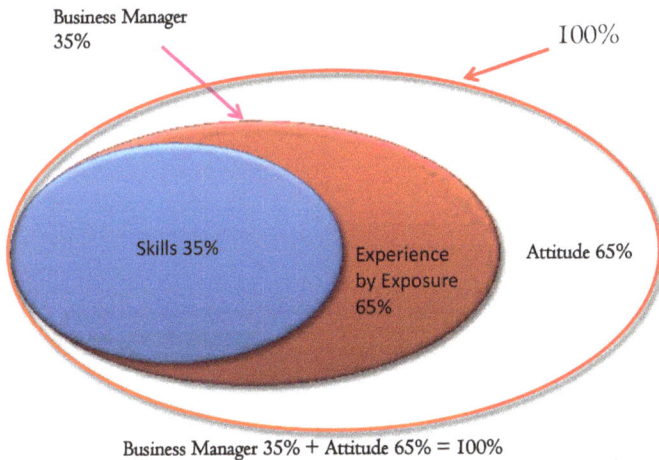

Business Manager
35%

100%

Skills 35%

Experience by Exposure 65%

Attitude 65%

Business Manager 35% + Attitude 65% = 100%

Gi – 26

A. BUSINESS-TYPE ENTREPRENEURS

1. Trading Entrepreneur

This entrepreneur engages in trading activities which can be regarded as part of the supply chain of the products involved. The business process includes procuring finished manufactured goods or services from the manufacturers or producer and selling directly to the consumer or through a retailer. The trading entrepreneur can also be the retailer at the tail end of the supply chain to the consumer. In this case the entrepreneur can be regarded as the middleman. The middleman between the manufacturer/producer and the dealer is the wholesaler, the middleman between the wholesaler and the retailer is simply referred to as the dealer while the middleman between the dealer and consumer is the retailer. The terms used to describe the middleman at different stages may vary from industry to industry. This type of entrepreneur generates many supplier-to-customer relationships along the supply chain.

2. Manufacturing Entrepreneur

The manufacturing entrepreneurs are producers of finished goods to satisfy the needs of customers. They identify and provide the capacity to convert necessary resources including technology and raw materials into finished desirable and sellable products.

3. Agricultural Entrepreneur

These are those entrepreneurs who engage in agricultural business. Their activities cover all aspects of agriculture and agricultural services. These include mechanisation, irrigation, farming, processing of produce, warehousing, marketing, merchandising and application of modern technology. An example is agricultural extension service to farmers whereby they receive training on modern farming methods, quality checks, harvesting, preservation and marketing.

B. TECHNOLOGY-TYPE ENTREPRENEURS

1. Technical Entrepreneur

These entrepreneurs businesses are science- and technology-based. They make use of science and technology in their enterprises and are known to easily adopt modern or innovative methods in their production.

2. Non-Technical Entrepreneur

These are entrepreneurs whose businesses are not directly technical based. Though most businesses nowadays use technology for communication, this type of entrepreneurs also use alternative imitative methods to market and distribute their products in the target market as a strategy to ensure that their businesses remain competitive and sustainable in the marketplace.

C. OWNERSHIP-BASED ENTREPRENEURS

1. Private Entrepreneur

This refers to sole proprietor of a business enterprise, usually setup by one owner. The sole owner of the enterprise takes all decisions concerning the business including financing, staffing, profit/loss and bears the entire risk involved in the business.

2. State Entrepreneur

This refers to a state or the government of a country engaging in trading especially in commodity or industrial venture. The common example is the oil producing countries directly involved in the sales of the crude oil and establishment of refineries through the state established agencies.

3. Joint Entrepreneur

Government of countries often enter into business agreement with companies, other than state entrepreneurs, having the required technical expertise and experience to transfer to a business establishment desired or already setup by the government. This agreement enables them to jointly run the business enterprise under a joint venture agreement. An example is the joint venture agreements between Nigerian National Petroleum Corporation (NNPC) and other oil exploring and marketing companies such as Shell, Exxon-Mobil etc.

D. GENDER-BASED ENTREPRENEUR

1. Men Entrepreneur

As the name implies, business enterprises that are owned, managed and controlled by men fall within this classification. This type is gradually phasing out as more and more of the opposite gender find the courage to venture into most business sectors.

2. Women Entrepreneur

Women entrepreneurs are so considered where the enterprise is owned and controlled by a woman or women. In addition, financial interest of the woman or women must be a minimum of 51% of the share capital and giving at least 51% of its employment to women.

E. SIZE-BASED ENTREPRENEURS

1. Small-scale Entrepreneur

An entrepreneur who has made investment in plant and machinery in accordance with the classification and categorisation of the locality of a reasonably small size will be referred to as a 'small-scale entrepreneur', usually a little over $10,000.

2.   Medium-scale Entrepreneur

The entrepreneur who has made investment in plant and machinery of usually above $25,000 can be classified as a 'medium-scale entrepreneur'. In Nigeria, Small and Medium Enterprises (SMEs) are those with sales or total assets not more than N4.5billion and having not more than 250 employees.

3.   Large-scale Entrepreneur

The entrepreneur who has made investment in plant and machinery of more than $50,000 is called a 'large-scale entrepreneur'.

F.   CIRCUMSTANTIAL ENTREPRENEURS

These are entrepreneurs that emerge with time in accordance with the societal need. They are capable of providing the right innovation for real-time economic transformation.

1.   Innovating Entrepreneur

Innovating entrepreneurs are those who introduce new goods, inaugurate new methods of production, discover new markets and reorganise the enterprise. These entrepreneurs bring changes to improve a development that already exists, to provide better solutions for the people in order to satisfy anticipated or their desire for improvement.

2. Imitative Entrepreneur

These are characterised by a readiness to adopt successful innovation inaugurated by innovating entrepreneurs. Imitative entrepreneurs provide similar solutions by using the innovative changes they adopted. They imitate techniques and technology innovated by others. This type of entrepreneur is peculiar to the underdeveloped regions where they provide imitation of new combinations of factors of production already existing in developed regions.

3. Fabian Entrepreneur

These entrepreneurs already exist, however, their scepticism and caution delay introduction of any change in their enterprises. A change is only adopted or imitated when it is absolutely clear that the enterprise may encounter great loss if they fail to do so.

4. Drone Entrepreneur

This type of entrepreneur is found in enterprises that flagrantly refuse to use visible opportunities to make changes in their production formulae and/or methods. They are highly prone to losses due to this insensitivity in comparison to their competitors.

G. BEHAVIOURAL-BASED ENTREPRENEURS

1. Solo Operator

Solo entrepreneurs are often individuals who essentially work alone where the individual's skills in the trade or profession and the competence are considered most vital for the product quality to offer the customer. Other services may be outsourced or employ a few employees to meet the demand of the business. Indeed, this presents the outlook of most start-ups.

2. Active Partner

These entrepreneurs start an enterprise as a joint venture and actively participate in the operation of the business. They are regarded as active partners because they share capital ownership by contribution of fund to the business as well as actively involved in running the enterprise. Entrepreneurs who are not actively involved in the operation of the business but only contribute funds to the capital are only partners but not active partners.

3. Inventor

These are those whose interest lies in research through which they invent new products. Their competence in inventiveness and innovative activities often lead to generation of new products. They are therefore regarded as inventors.

4.   Challenger

These entrepreneurs are attracted by challenges into industry because of the challenges it presents. They satiate for challenges such that when one challenge is met, they quickly search out new challenges to be met.

5.   Buyer

These entrepreneurs are peculiar in their type because they hardly start up new enterprise but rather buy up an existing one. They opted for this option in order to lower the risk they will have to bear with a start-up and therefore prefer to buy an existing one. It should also be noted that entrepreneurs among other types may at any point, in addition, choose to be a buyer entrepreneur, whereby an acquisition of an existing enterprise is involved. An example is Mark Zuckerburg of Face Book acquisition of WhatsApp.

6.   Life-Timer

Business is integrated into the life of this type of entrepreneur. Most businesses which heavily depend on personal skills and mastery belong here. Family businesses that are based on generational skills transfer are also of this type of entrepreneur.

ENTERPRISE

An enterprise is the main body of a business that encompasses all the organs, processes, resources, activities and identity. It is a legal entity established for the purpose of business in a known environment or community and as such is recognised to exist under the legal framework of the region.

The entrepreneurs or persons who establish the enterprise shall organise the necessary resources for the performance of business activities and generation of benefits such as profit, recognition and goodwill.

A solo entrepreneur can own an idea suitable to address specific or generic need in a non-saturated market which is eventually developed into an enterprise by registering a company name only with one business owner for the purpose of generating business activities through the registered enterprise. The entrepreneur must source, provide, and organise all resources to produce, promote and offer the products from the production process of the organisation, in this case, a micro-enterprise, due to the size of its structure.

The enterprise must be established and operated in accordance with the regulatory guidelines of the country, county or state and sometimes including the local authority where it is located. The requirement may include filing or submission of periodic business reports of the enterprise to the designated authority such as company income tax returns to the Federal Inland Revenue Services (FIRS) and annual company reports to the Corporate Affairs Commission (CAC) in the case of Nigeria.

The enterprises are classified into micro, small, medium and large scales depending on the criteria applied and the region under consideration.

3

The Creative Entrepreneur and Manager

Creative Entrepreneurs

Gi – 27

"The creative entrepreneur is mostly a creative person
with initiatives that provide solutions to anticipated
customers' needs"

———————

Author

———————

Who is a Creative Entrepreneur?

From the earlier chapters, the creative entrepreneur can be viewed as:

- The creative entrepreneur is mostly a creative person with initiatives to use creativity to offer solutions to anticipated needs of customers within and outside the region of his enterprise.

- A person whose activities in the creative sector encompass business processes under the identity of an enterprise with evident business success or potential to generate benefits from those activities.

- The creative entrepreneur is a business owner, competent organiser and manager of resources to generate desired benefits for growth and sustainability of a business in the sector.

- The products on offer are often unique and offer aesthetics, beauty and attractiveness to the customer with potential for increment in value.

- Some offer their creative services to provide designs that are adopted for industrial purposes. This is available in the fashion and furniture industries.

- Some are pure innovators and engage mainly in research, design and redesign of styles, forms and figures for the use of other entrepreneurs.

Qualities of a Creative Entrepreneur

1. Entrepreneurial Ability

- Self-driven Passion: This is the foremost quality that sets a creative entrepreneur apart from others as the application of creative talent drives the pace and reach the entrepreneur desires to spread the product of the creativity. As a result, creative product from this entrepreneur reaches the customers through the deployment of appropriate marketing strategy.
- Enterprise Management: The entrepreneur must ensure the proper management of the enterprise. All resources of the enterprise must be given adequate organisation with the provision of monitoring, control, auditing, appraisal and renewals as may be deemed necessary. There will also be periodic reports that must be properly directed for the purpose of protection of the integrity of the company. In addition, the entrepreneur must prepare for decision times concerning fund management, employee size, collaborations, expansion and a few others that may become inevitable.
- Communication: There is no gainsaying that the ability to communicate effectively at all times will eliminate failures in the processes and the business of the entrepreneur in general. Communication to remain up-to-date in the profession will require networking in the right forums with the right group of people physically and through the use of technology. Corporate communication is essential in order to maintain corporate integrity

with the regulatory authorities in the region, such as mentioned earlier, will keep the business in the good books of the authorities. Business success rests in the turnover and the market share controlled by the enterprise of the entrepreneur, hence, marketing communication is of utmost importance for maintaining good business performance and sustainability. While the entrepreneur is also encouraged to establish communication with allied entrepreneurs on desirable collaboration for mutual benefits.

2. New Business Innovation

- Many creative entrepreneurs have tendency to innovate bringing out new ideas and new products. The innovation often adopted by industrial customers who use them to produce new goods into the market. Their innovation therefore creates economic value while providing social solutions.
- However, creative entrepreneurs who are solo entrepreneurs will usually innovate and also be responsible for marketing their own products. This they often do directly or through agents.

3. Leadership

Leadership ability: To lead in the sector, the creative entrepreneur must be visionary and exhibit good leadership skills, which inspire others and attract them to follow in the vision, or be motivated to use their talents for value addition in the enterprise of the leader or the sector. The strength of the influence the entrepreneur impacts in the sector signifies the recognition that will be attracted. This is usually evident when creativity awards are offered to deserving awardees in the sector.

Social Responsibility: The creative entrepreneur has the ability to add value to the community, through efforts aimed at identifying local problems, and enabling solutions, using acceptable means of interventions. This may be through isolated enterprise or joint approach within the sector. In most cases benefiting localities or communities within the market will reciprocate the gesture for a win-win benefit such as promoting peaceful coexistence and enabling conducive business environment for the enterprise and the sector.

4. Knowledge of the Market

- Each market has its own peculiarity; the creative entrepreneur needs to study the local terrain and get sensitive to the peculiarity, knowing which enables the development of strategic marketing approach to acquire the desired level of customer size in the market.
- The creative entrepreneur can also identify need gaps that may serve as opportunity to generate further creative solutions and grow the business in the market.

THE CREATIVE ENTREPRENEUR A - Z

EDUCATION AND CONTINUOUS TRAINING REQUIREMENT TOWARDS SUCESSFUL ENTREPRENEUERSHIP

BASIC SKILLS	35%	SUPPORT COMPLEMENTARY EDUCATION REQUIREMENT	65%
- Conceptual And Design Skills Developed	15%	- Politics - Local And Global Knowledge	10%
- Drawings and Presentation	10%	- Business Management - Office/Practice Administration - Operations Management	10%
- Contract Documentation	10%	- Networking/Marketing Through Strategic Partners - Need Assessment	10%
		- Procurement	10%
		- Finance/Accounts - Project/Office Administration	10%
		- Project Management - Knowledge Of Other Services	10%
		- Others	5%
	35%		65%

HUMANITIES   ARTS & DESIGN CREATIVITY   SCIENCE   TECHNOLOGY

Gi - 28

The basic entrepreneur deploys talent, skills and development towards the realisation of a successful enterprise.

The above is a typical development model for an architect and can also serve a creative entrepreneur with a slight adjustment based on actual need.

4
Setting up and Managing Enterprises

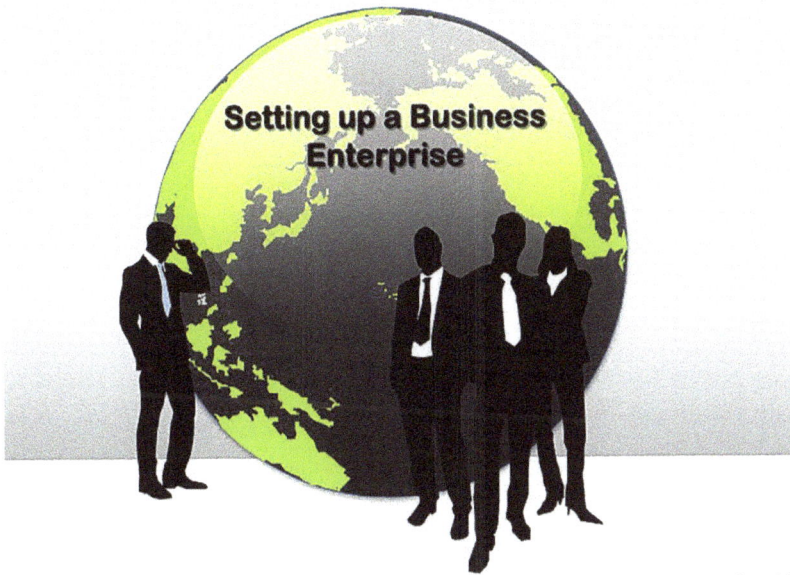

Setting up a Business Enterprise

Gi - 29

"Entrepreneurial acumens, unbeatable business ideas, commercial insight and business savvy keep an enterprise out of eviction"

Ogwu Sunday

SETTING UP AND MANAGING ENTERPRISES

1. Preparing Business Plan

The entrepreneur prepares a statement called a 'business plan' or 'project report' of what is proposed to take up at start-up and later for development of the business. In other words, a business plan is a well-evolved course of action designed by the entrepreneur to achieve the specified objectives within a specified period of time.

In this sense, a business plan is just like an operating document. The preparation of a business plan is very useful for the entrepreneur to establish the enterprise in an effective and smooth manner. It is a vital instrument for seeking financial assistance from the banks and other financial institutions for the enterprises.

It contains information about the intending business owner or owners, vision and mission statements, location of the enterprise, requirement for land and building, plant and machinery, raw materials, utilities, transport and communication, digital information systems, manpower, requirement for funds with projected working capital, sources of funds, projected cash flow statement and statement of financial position for the first three years, break-even point, organisational structure, marketing, and implementation plan of the business to include implementation schedule when a project is involved.

2. Decision-Making

The entrepreneur is responsible for all policy decisions of the business, including staffing, buying or leasing, production level, promotion, borrowing etc. Guiding by the set production policy, an entrepreneur determines what to produce, how much to produce, how to produce, where to produce, how to sell, and so forth. Moreover, he decides the scale of production and the proportion in which he combines the different factors he employs. In brief, he has to make vital business decisions relating to the purchase of productive factors and to the sale of the finished goods or services. Same applies in the case of other set policies, employee policy, finance policy etc.

3. Management Control

The entrepreneur has to manage and set up monitoring systems to control the running of the business and ensure good performance. So, he must possess a high degree of management ability to directly or through outsourcing recruit the right type of personnel for the business. He is also responsible for setting up the appropriate style and type of management control that will suit his enterprise.

4. Division of Income

The next major function of the entrepreneur is to make necessary arrangements for the division of total income among the different factors of production employed by him. Even if there is a loss in the business, he has to pay rent, interest, wages and other contractual outgoings from the realised sale proceeds or project fees. The entrepreneur prepares the requirement for funds with its detailed structure. The financial requirement is classified separately into short-term and long-term according to the enterprise finance policy. The preferred sources of the required funds are then considered. How much capital will be borrowed from different financial institutions and banks are clearly determined. A finance expert or chartered accountant will be able to provide useful information. Notwithstanding finance expert guidance, the entrepreneur takes full responsibility for the final outcome.

5.   Risk-Taking and Uncertainty-Bearing

Entrepreneurship is characterised by risk-taking. This is a key factor or the most important function an entrepreneur performs. Modern production is very risky, as an entrepreneur is required to produce goods or services in anticipation of their future demand.

Risk-bearing is inevitable in business. There are two major kinds of risk that should be of concern to the entrepreneur. The first is the measurable kind, these are insurable and include, fire, theft, accidents, loss of goods in transit, professional indemnity etc. The second kind of risk cannot be anticipated with measurable certainty and so, cannot be insured against, because their probability cannot be calculated accurately. These constitute what is called uncertainty. They include competition risk, technical risk, natural disaster etc. The entrepreneur faces both kinds of risk in the business.

6. Innovation

Another function that distinguishes an entrepreneur is innovation. The entrepreneur brings forth new ideas, new strategies as well as invention of new products, new techniques and discovering new markets, to improve the competitive position of the enterprise, and to increase earnings.

7. Organising

The organising function of an entrepreneur refers to bringing together the people, material, machinery, money, etc., to execute the plans. The entrepreneur assembles and organises the above-mentioned different organs of an enterprise in such a way that these combine to start functioning as one, i.e. enterprise. Thus, the organising function of an entrepreneur ultimately provides a mechanism for purposeful, integrated and co-operative action by many people in a joint and organised effort to implement a business plan.

8. Staffing

It is generally believed that the employees of an enterprise hold the key to its success. This makes employee selection very vital in the decision of the entrepreneur, in order to have the right calibre of personnel most suitable for different roles or positions of responsibilities. Thus, the staffing function of an entrepreneur includes identifying the number and characteristics of personnel available, which initially will be the entrepreneur only, determining the job roles for the business, assessing the required number and characteristics of personnel, carry out manpower recruitment including selection, remuneration, training and development, and periodic appraisal of personnel working in the enterprise.

The importance of the role of personnel in the success of an organisation is highly rated. This is supported by the statement of renowned business scientists, L. F. Urwick who remarked that, "business houses are made or broken in the long-run not by markets or capital, patents or equipment, but by men." And, Andrew Carniege's view that "take my people and leave my factory, soon grass will grow on the floor. Take my factory and leave my people, soon we shall build a better factory." This also emphasises the significance of proper staffing in the making of an organisation to drive performance. However, the staffing function is equally as crucial as it is complex for the success of a business enterprise.

9.   Production/Manufacturing

Once the enterprise is finally established, it starts producing goods or offering services, whichever is the case. Manufacturing requires a factory for production of the goods as a vital activity of the value chain.

Therefore, this will include decisions relating to the selection of factory site, design and layout, production machinery, types of products to be produced, research and development, and design of the product.

The ancillary activities include production planning and control, maintenance and repair, purchasing, store-keeping, supply and material handling. The effective performance of production function in manufacturing business, to a large extent, depends on the proper production planning and control.

Services on the other hand may be rendered physically at a workshop, an office or even virtually via the internet depending on the service on offer. Examples are many digital applications, Apps or Applets that are downloadable by online subscription.

10. Marketing

An enterprise produces goods or services which are basically meant for the market. Marketing activities direct the flow of goods and services from producer to consumer or user. Marketing essentially identifies consumer needs, establishes consumer behaviour, communicates the needs and other relative information including competition, to the enterprise, as well as communicates new development that meets the needs to the consumer. Therefore, marketing can be said to begin and end with the customers. It is important to note that selling is though the last function in marketing activities, it is when the deal is converted to sale that the marketing becomes effective and company income and performance appreciate.

Other marketing activities include market or consumer research, product planning and development, standardisation, packaging, pricing, storage, promotional activities, distribution channel development and management, etc. The success of the marketing function of an enterprise depends largely on the appropriate combination the 'marketing mix', formerly known as 4Ps, namely: product, price, promotion, and place and later expanded to 7Ps as packaging, people, and process are added to the marketing mix.

11. Accounting

Accounting is a service most desirable to provide a business enterprise with information about its financial performance. This involves only activities that can be measured in monetary terms. The information is provided for specified period usually a year and will show the performance of the business based on the expenditure against income generated. Therefore, what is accounting and what impact does it make on the enterprise? Most proponents of accounting agree that, accounting provides information about the financial performance of an entity meaning an enterprise, and its assets and liabilities to those who need it. This enables informed decisions to be made by the users of the information.

Accounting is divided into two main functions, namely: I. Financial accounting, which deals in keeping and classification of financial records and preparation of financial statements such as statement of financial position, cash flow statement etc. for the use of external stakeholders in accordance with appropriate accounting standards and principles as well as in line with legal requirement. Such information is usually provided during and at the end of an established accounting period. 2. Management accounting, still based on the application of the principles of accounting and financial management, includes creating, protecting, increasing and preserving value for the business. The latter function is usually part of internal management and responsible for generation of relevant information for strategic planning, funding, planning and control and a host of others. Management accounting takes a closer view of the inflow and outflow of the business process and includes cost management. This subject is detailed in subsequent chapters in view of its importance in the success of an enterprise.

5

Finance, Accounts and Taxes

Gi - 30

"You either know how finance and accounting work in your enterprise or you are inviting the doom!"

_____

Anonymous

_____

FINANCE, ACCOUNTS AND TAXES

One of the resources of the enterprise is money which is used to fund its existence. This chapter looks at the role the entrepreneur must play to ensure that the enterprise remains relevant, operational and sustained in the marketplace based on how funds are managed. Davoren suggested that companies must ensure that all aspects of accounting exist and correctly managed to ensure competitiveness adequate liquidity. Those entrepreneurs who embrace this approach in their businesses are most likely to continuously flourish.

1.   Finance

In simple sense, this is the management of funds for an enterprise encompassing function including: effective sourcing, injecting, generating, distribution, usage, monitoring, controlling, recording, analysing, reporting and so on, to ensure that the funds of the enterprise are correctly utilised for profitability, thus assuring continuous operation, business growth, meeting competition, increasing market share and sustainability of the enterprise.

An enterprise derives funding from three key sources, these are, revenues from sales/service, investors' finances including owners, partners or venture capital, and loans obtained from individuals, or financial organisations. There is need to have adequate funding to remain in business, therefore, the working capital comprising cash inflow and outflow, the holding stock or inventory as well as the receivables from customers and payables to creditors which contribute significantly to the liquidity of the enterprise must be handled with firm decisiveness. Maintaining liquidity and profitable business will enable the enterprise honour its short term liabilities including employee remuneration, payment to creditors etc. and long term expenses such as purchase of plant and machinery, repayment of loan, purchase of land and buildings etc.

Certain policies for strengthening liquidity must be put in place such as credit policy and discount policy applicable to customers, ensuring credit worthiness of a customer prior approval of credit sale, on the other hand, common payment terms that are set out in the procurement policy to avoid liquidity challenges include: thirty days end of the month (30EoM) meaning that payment will be made thirty days starting from end of the month of supply to the enterprise, also, sixty days end of the month (60EoM) meaning that the payment will be made sixty days starting from the end of the month of supply of material or services to the enterprise. When the supplier is aware and consent to these terms, they will only expect payment in line with the policy of their customer.

There are unavoidable risks such as accident, vehicle, professional indemnity (for professional services entrepreneurs) etc. that limit flow of revenue and can negatively affect the level of funds available to the business. This must be anticipated and adequately insured with appropriate coverage.

Internal controls must be strategically designed and importantly effective at elimination of loopholes and untoward conducts that can affect both the funds and the existence of the business. The frequency and style will depend on the complexity of the finance processes involved.

Cash budget is very useful for planning, for the forecast of outflow of money (payments) and the amount of finances needed to meet those outflows.

2. Long-Term Requirements

Long-term goals require long term funds. Replacing plants or machinery, new buildings, expanding into new territories are long-term projects that cannot be realised with short-term funds. Finance shortage from short-term sources could repeatedly hinder these projects. Long-term projects should be financed with business savings (retained earnings) or bank loans. Capital budgeting and proper planning can be used to estimate when your long-term expenses would occur.

3. Financial Goals

Financial goal is a strong factor that the entrepreneur addresses repeatedly and strategises on, based on the financial resources available to meet the financial objectives of the business at various periods. The goals in other areas of the business shape the financial goal. These include: scaling up production capacity to increase production and reduce production cost, increasing sales by financing promotion and offering discounts. Repayment of principal amount and interest on loans used to finance the business and giving attractive returns to investors' for their funds may be key objectives of the financial goals.

4. Accounting

Core to the success of any business enterprise is the Method of Accounting for the business. It is very important for an entrepreneur to give serious attention to accounting to ensure the primary objective of profit maximisation is achieved.

The Entrepreneur should be able to identify and classify the business in such a way that Profit should be distinguished from Revenue, Capital from Asset and Liability. At least, the knowledge of book-keeping, the basic operation in accounting is required by every entrepreneur.

The business dictionary defines Accounting as: "Practice and body of knowledge concerned primarily with methods for recording transactions, keeping financial records, performing internal audits, reporting and analysing financial information to the management, and advising on taxation matters."

Gi - 32

In other words, accounting provides financial information that enables the entrepreneur make informed decision. The process to achieve this includes recording of all financial transactions, measuring, recording and classifying them as well as summarising and interpreting them for management use. Importantly, the profit or loss for the period will be evident in the report, and also, the enterprise assets, liabilities and the equity of the owners.

The department handles the financial aspects of the business and can be said to manage the economic front of any business or enterprise and therefore must be maintained efficiently. It is concerned with the resources available to an enterprise, how the resources are financed, and the results from their use. The records of payments, receipts, credits and debts are kept and updated in the department.

Accounting must not be overlooked even though the department runs its operations mostly behind-the-scenes, as opposed to departments like Marketing, Purchasing and Human Resource Management, which deal with front-line business activities. However, a success-driven entrepreneur knows the value of an efficient accounting system to the enterprise.

5.   Functions of Accountants

Accountants provide various diverse financial services to the company. The list of functions include: recording accounts payable and receivable, payroll, procurement and inventory, property accounts and all other financial elements. The most important is that all records must be analysed and summarised and various reports developed with useful information for various stakeholders use to make informed decisions.

6. Payroll

Calculation of salaries and wages and other benefits that accrue to staff and periodic payment to the employees is entrusted to the account department. The department is tasked to ensure that all employees receive a fair pay, including bonuses, commissions, and other benefits. Workers' annual leave, casual leave, off days, and sick leave are also taken into consideration.

The payroll calculation requires access to personnel remuneration information for each staff and therefore must maintain a copy for their record and update as soon as any change occurs. This information is used to calculate the amount of individual staff income tax, pension contribution, social security tax, union fees to be deducted. In addition, salary advances (IOU) will be deducted if applicable. All deductions are from gross earnings before the take-home pay to each employee is arrived at. Taxes deducted from employee salary, and company contributions, payable to the state and federal government by the company have to be calculated and updated.

Business expenses incurred by employees may be reimbursed through the payroll depending on the policy of the enterprise.

7. Cash Inflows

This refers to all moneys received by the business for the period under consideration, including revenue from sales, payments from debtors, discounts from suppliers, etc. They are identified and entered into cash book in the books of account and the balance against company expenses determined. It is important to keep detailed and accurate records of all incoming revenues of any magnitude.

A sound process of tracking debtors and receipts of payments of their outstanding invoices must be closely managed. Each debtor's account must be updated regularly and reminder sent to them, if necessary, to ensure that customers pay their invoices on time. A correct cash inflow record will contribute to realistic determination of the enterprise's annual profit or loss.

8. Cash Outflows

This is the statement of all types of expenses incurred by the business over a referred period. The day-to-day running cost falls into this. Others are purchase account record for direct materials, plant and machinery, vehicle, stamp and postages, salaries and wages, taxes, travels and tours, training, land and buildings, rent, telephone, utilities, repairs and maintenance, repayment of loans and many more. These outflows are paid by various means including, bank transfer, telegraphic transfer, cheques or cash. The cash request must be prepared, by the account department, for the request of the fund to meet the payment each time it occurs for proper recording and retrieval for future use.

To maintain good business reputation, the enterprise must honour its obligation with timely payment of its debts to its suppliers at all times. Fast payment is advisable for discount offered, whereas late payment charges are costly and so must be avoided.

There are many genuine ways to cut costs. The accounting department must always be ahead in negotiation of suitable discounts and contra deals for the business, to ensure that the inputs demand less cash and are of required quality that can generate the desired output product quality and quantity.

CASH INFLOW

CASH OUTFLOW

CASH Flows

9. Inventory

An inventory also called stock comprises the products (semi-finished goods, finished goods and goods in-transit) and supplies (raw materials) of an enterprise which are ultimately converted to sale with the aim of being sold within a year. It is important to keep accurate inventory records. Hence, the most suitable inventory pricing method has to be applied from the available options of: last-in-first-out cost (LIFO), weighted-average cost (AVCO) or first-in-first-out cost (FIFO). This is to forestall adverse effect of input cost on the cash flow. The inventory must also be balanced at all times at level that is cost-effective and sufficient to keep customers satisfied.

10. Fixed Assets and Property Accounting

Fixed assets are tangible assets and are often owned by the business over a long period of time and cannot easily be converted to cash. They include land and buildings, plant and machinery, vehicles, etc. Businesses require increasing their assets when a decision to increase production capacity has been taken by the owners.

Fixed assets are managed with appropriate depreciation method for each type. Proper record and levels of depreciation must be maintained at all times for controlling the use of the assets, determination of taxes payable to authorities, and included in the balance sheet (statement of financial position) showing the total company assets, liabilities and capital for a reported period.

The accounting department must ensure that the company's financial statements are kept up-to-date.

The entrepreneur can rely on the financial statements like the profit and loss account (comprehensive income statement) and the balance sheet, to know the overall worth and value of the enterprise. This can guide the decision for actions that will keep the business more competitive in the market for the next period.

The accounting department may be assigned other related works as well, but this is a comprehensive list of its major functions. The significance of these functions in running the business is enormous. An entrepreneur must understand that paying employees accurately and on time, keeping detailed records (accounts) of assets and liabilities, and of income and expenditure are key drivers of business success and continuity.

For overall business efficiency, the accounting department must perform these functions effectively and timely, by applying the proper accounting standards and procedures as well as maintaining detailed and up-to-date records at all times.

IMPORTANCE OF THE ACCOUNTING DEPARTMENT TO AN ENTERPRISE

The importance of the accounting department stems from its role in maintaining the enterprise's financial operation. The department records and keeps the records of all business transactions which are usually in monetary terms and can be classified as income or expenditure. Ensuring that the accounting department remains focused, committed and effective on its roles and delivers a robust and efficient accounting can assist to score the enterprise's performance high in all criteria.

Reporting Line and Span of Control in an Accounting Department

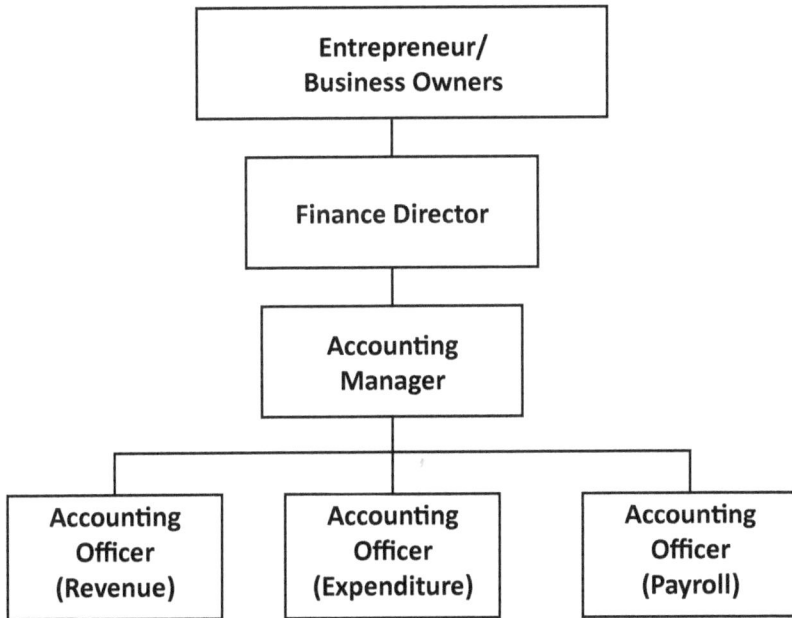

```
┌─────────────────────────┐
│   Entrepreneur/         │
│   Business Owners       │
└─────────────────────────┘
           │
┌─────────────────────────┐
│   Finance Director      │
└─────────────────────────┘
           │
┌─────────────────────────┐
│   Accounting            │
│   Manager               │
└─────────────────────────┘
```

| Accounting Officer (Revenue) | Accounting Officer (Expenditure) | Accounting Officer (Payroll) |

Gi - 34

The chart represents the model for a medium to large enterprise with all levels occupied by Accounting Professionals. The entrepreneur can modify the chart according to the size of the business, whereby, the accounting officer position is occupied by an accounting expert who reports directly to the business owner / entrepreneur of a micro to small enterprise.

1.   Cost-Cutting

The input of accounting department in determination of costs and identifying areas to cut costs without adversely affecting the operations of the enterprise makes cost-cutting a key area in accounting function. By being the custodian of financial statements and company costs, the accounting department has the knowledge of where the business can reduce costs. The information to the management and other departments can lead to strategies that will lead to higher profitability and shareholders wealth.

2.   Cost-Effectiveness

The information provided to the management by the accounting department, including the financial data helps the management or the individual affected managers' make useful, well informed business decisions and further control usage of the company assets and other resources.

The department provides details of cost incurred by the business and their payback in certain areas, such as, direct labour cost versus goods produced, the return from sales versus marketing, advertising and distribution, etc. The enterprise's operations which are most cost-effective are identified and maintained while the least cost-effective are modified. The department can also advise on the feasibility of proposed business ventures or new projects such as expansion, mergers, and takeovers, by developing feasibility report that informs the management or the entrepreneur on viability before final decision.

3. Influencing Financial Decisions

The financial records prepared by the accounting department are useful to various external stakeholders, including shareholders, state and federal governments, creditors, debtors, banks, etc., for important decisions that they may have to make about the enterprise. These decisions may do with lending large sums to the enterprise by banks or other financial institutions, or offering significant amount of credit by creditors (suppliers); investing decisions are made by prospective investors (shareholders and stockholders). Income tax and other taxes payable to government agencies can be determined using the information. When seeking to obtain credits and/or investments, the enterprise can be helped with the financial information from accounting department.

4.   Effective Financial Strategies

By reviewing the past financial decisions, accounting department prepares a recommended budget, while considering the company's objectives and the entrepreneur's or managers' decisions, highlighting areas that require focus to increase business efficiency. The department monitors the deployment of the strategy and the changes realised by the business when the strategy is in effect.

The function of the accounting department touches the overall operations of the business. This puts the department in advisory position and can advise the entrepreneur on the performance of the business at any point and the required changes that may be needed.

THE SET-UP OF AN ACCOUNTING DEPARTMENT

An accounting department should be set-up with careful consideration. A company's accounting system is key in determining its overall success. The accounting system changes with time and may vary from region to region. Technology changes and influence on accounting demands that today's accounting department must be set up with computerised accounting. It is more time- and cost-effective, it occupies less space and requires less labour as compared to the manual alternative. The following steps are recommended for the set-up of an accounting department:

1. Hire an Accountant

For every entrepreneur that is not in the business of finance and accounting or an accountant by profession, the first question to ask is, am I competent to adequately prepare the required financial reports of my enterprise for the various purposes and diverse stakeholders who use these reports? If your answer is no, then you must hire an accountant, even on freelance engagement, at the least for micro business or set up an accounting department for small business upwards. While most entrepreneurs, based on their business acumen have the ability to keep records, they are not likely to be very clear and detailed due to shortage of know-how on prioritising, documenting, classifying, recording, analysing, summarising financial data that lead to those reports, which may consequently lead to incorrect information and poor decision making at the detriment of their enterprises' performance. Therefore, when considering the composition of an enterprise's human resources, it is advisable to include an accountant for micro business or accounting department for small business upwards.

2. Select an Accounting Method

There are two accounting methods to be considered, depending on the simplicity or complexity of the transactions expected from the business, and based on the size of the enterprise.

Cash-basis accounting method: This is the simpler method whereby income is only recorded when cash is received and expenses recorded when the payments are made. Mostly found with micro and some small enterprises that pay for goods and services immediately and generate their income similarly when goods are sold and as soon as they offer a service. It is very reliable for tracking the actual amount of money being received and being spent at every point in time.

Accrual accounting: This method refers to when income and expenditure are recorded as soon as goods are sold or a purchase is made respectively, regardless of whether actual money is received or paid for the transactions. It is more suitable for enterprises that buy and/or sell goods and services on credit. The main benefit of this method is that it helps the enterprise to know how much income is realised alongside the expenditure on monthly basis and the profit it is generating.

The accrual accounting method is more favourable and commonly used by businesses, especially small to large enterprises.

Choosing Method for Recording Transactions

There are two methods for recording transactions into the accounts. These are manual recording and automated recording. An entrepreneur will have to choose, usually with professional guidance, capacity and volume of the business, the more suitable of the available options.

Manual recording: A manual ledger is provided into which the accountants hand-writes. This is not very common anymore due to being a time consuming, intensive operation when large numbers of transactions have to be entered daily in a ledger. In addition it is highly prone to errors which can lead to misinformation for the enterprise and thus misleading. However, some microenterprises with moderate number of transactions still adopt this method conveniently without adverse effect.

Automated recording: This offers electronic recording of transactions using a software program in a computer. It is simpler and able to process large data arising from several transactions with high level of accuracy. With it, the performance of routine, periodic and other tasks are quick, efficient and more reliable such that errors due to discrepancies or inconsistencies in the accounts can be tracked and easily corrected.

TAXATION

Taxes are levies imposed on individuals and corporations by the government, where they are located or operating. This may include the local, state or federal (central) government. The enterprise must be a limited liability company, in accordance with entity rule in accounting to be levied, while a sole trader enterprise is not subject to corporation tax but the owner is taxed directly from the profit earned over a year period. Tax is what the government uses to finance its expenditure and to implement its fiscal policy.

The enterprise is responsible for the deduction of personal income tax from the employees and remits to the government. It is also expected to pay corporation tax on its business at the end of every tax year. To have an effective tax strategy and be successful, every enterprise must have knowledge of the applicable tax laws and pragmatically use credits that are inherent in the tax code. Tax policy must include tax planning to benefit from tax avoidance which may reduce tax liability, thereby increase profitability. The enterprise must also ensure full disclosure to avoid the bitter consequences of tax evasion.

Importance of Tax Planning

Tax planning is a strategy that when effectively employed, helps to minimise tax liabilities through use of the opportunity that tax credits in the tax code offer businesses. This is of benefits to all sizes of enterprise that are of entity status. With tax planning the enterprise can optimise the tax relief and credits available, thereby, lower amount of taxable income, reduce tax rate, have greater control of when tax gets paid.

Tax planning should be reviewed as soon as new changes occur in the tax code which usually affects the allowances.

Types of Tax Planning Strategies

Tax planners are very useful professionals for guiding enterprises on up-to-date information pertaining to taxation. They are closer to the changes than most entrepreneurs or the managers of their businesses except in large enterprises where the tax planner is an officer engaged within the organisation. The strategies are basically of benefit for reducing tax liability and include as follows:

1. Capital Gains Tax Planning

Capital gain tax is not a trading or income tax. It refers to the levy on the chargeable gain resulting from the sale or disposal of an asset and is normally regulated by specific tax legislation. Entrepreneurs will get useful advice from tax experts on possible reliefs and exemptions to minimise the tax amount. Tax planners can identify the likelihood of capital loss from the asset disposal proceeds to be set against capital gain. The tax planners can also identify and state those assets that are affected and those that are exempt and calculate the liability for the enterprise or individual entrepreneur as may be appropriate.

2. Corporate Tax Planning

Corporate tax as the name implies is mandatory to all business entities and considered as large cost to profitable enterprises. However, more profit can be retained with very effective corporate tax planning by all sizes of enterprises, enabling them reduce their corporate tax liabilities. Capital allowances and Calculations based on the accruals' concept using deferred credit and deferred income and profits are part of the strategies in practice for corporate tax planning. In certain countries, new enterprises can benefit from tax holiday, a period, usually over a few years, when a business is allowed not to pay tax to the government.

International Tax Planning

Similar to corporate tax planning and others, International Tax planning is fundamental to reducing tax liability and keeping more part of the profit for the business. Strategies including tax deferral, avoiding double or multiple taxation, foreign tax credits, tax haven and scheduling tax bills are helpful for minimising foreign tax liabilities.

1. Year-end Tax Planning

To hold a significant profit in the enterprise's business during a year, a large dividend may be drawn out of the profit for the shareholders, especially when they comprise mainly of employees and the entrepreneur, and its payment deferred. The advice for the most tax-efficient way to make the payment can be obtained from the tax expert.

2. Tax Consultants

Tax consultants are certified professionals and experts in managing tax matters and related issues. Their services include: tax planning, expert advice on different types of taxes and the strategies to minimise tax liabilities and protect wealth.

6 Investors and Investing in Enterprises

Gi - 35

Every entrepreneur should take decision based on calculated risk: "Win some and let others go."

———————

Author

———————

INVESTORS AND INVESTING IN ENTERPRISES

The investor(s) is or are persons or organisations that already have access to wealth in the form of cash or assets and are capable of deploying such assets for possible growth. The most usual place for such investment is usually with an enterprise which could be a business venture in production, service, banking or other sectors.

The entrepreneur will require some form of investment by investors for the enterprise to succeed.

Therefore, it behoves that the investor and the entrepreneur are the most desirable for job and wealth creation to succeed.

Whereas the entrepreneur identifies the right opportunity, the investor views his effort from the perspective of entry and investment and a smooth exit with profit.

A handshake before, during and after signifies the satisfaction of all.

Can entrepreneurs continue to dominate the Forbes list of wealthiest people? In actual fact, that is possible and may be long standing unbroken record, based on the entrepreneurs' zeal to retain earnings, attract more funds from investors (their rival in wealth comparison) and invest in fixed assets among other needs for the realisation of strategic business goals such as: increase production capacity, expand into new market, diversification, etc. The profit realised will benefit both the investor and the entrepreneur to increase their liquid assets. The difference between both is that, the entrepreneur multiplies the funds from investors to generate the profit that increases the liquid assets of both while the entrepreneur has the advantage to retain the fixed assets in the enterprise, which thereby increase the net worth that translates to the wealth of the entrepreneur.

The entrepreneurs who will continue to excel in this manner are those who make concerted effort to deploy entrepreneurial characteristics at best.

The meeting point of creativity deployment is in entrepreneurship knowledge, ability and capability.

A well-co-ordinated creative industry entrepreneur will be capable of providing the right investors' confidence and guarantee for their investment.

The resultant effect is an effective job and wealth creation, providing a vibrant, stable economy for the nation. It is therefore paramount for the creative entrepreneur to have the right knowledge of investment and deployment of same to effective productivity for profit and sustainability.

7

Strategic ideas on how to build a new business

"Successful entrepreneurs have the unique ability to organize and achieve sustainable value for all stakeholders"

———

Enesi Makoju

———

TEN STRATEGIC IDEAS ON HOW TO BUILD A NEW BUSINESS

Gi - 36

1. Business type identification

2. Make Business Plan

3. Plan your finances

4. Choose a business structure

5. Register business name

6. Licences and permits

7. Accounting system

8. Business location

9. Work team/employees

10. Promotion, launching and marketing

1. Business Type Identification

The most common approach to building a new business is for the entrepreneur to focus on his personal skill. However, in order for a business to be successful, it must solve a problem, fulfil a need or offer something the market wants.

These can be identified by either research works or a deep plunge into the trial and error method. A fair knowledge of the need for products/services, who needs it and whether or not there exist other companies offering the same is also a necessity. Whichever the case may be, what you offer either as a complement or an improvement to what exists will determine how successful your business enterprise will be.

2. Make a Business Plan

A business plan should be considered paramount in new business set-ups. A business plan is a blueprint that will guide your business from start-up stage through establishment and eventual business growth. There are different types of business plans which, in general principles, will depend on the intended set-up approach.

Whereas the traditional business plan will be for guidance on A to Z, the more comprehensive will enable the involvement of the would-be investors, or at least make it easy to seek financial support from banks and financial institutions. These plans will probably need to be reviewed over time as the enterprise develops.

3. Plan Your Finances

The smartest way to start a business is to limit the initial capital input to the barest minimum; costs must be reviewed, with suitable options for sustainability. The services of an accountant can be sought to develop a spread-sheet that estimates the one-time start-up cost of your business, as well as what you anticipate you will need to keep your business running for at least 12 months (rent, utilities, marketing and advertising, employee salaries, etc.) as a follow-up to your business plan.

4. Choose a Business Structure

Chapter 4 gives a vivid illustration of the most suitable enterprise type and category. You will have to decide on business type as, a sole proprietorship, a partnership or limited liability company or corporation.

The business type chosen will have a bearing on the eventual business name, your liability and filing tax returns.

The business structure can be modified as need arises for making a case for transformation to accommodate other participants or players, such as investors or franchise.

5.   Business Name

The choice of a business name will depend on several factors. Whatever the case may be, it should reflect your business type and model as much as possible. In some cases you could be creating a partnership or franchise, or you may be adopting an already existing name brand.

Once you have chosen a name, you will need to register it with the appropriate authority. It may also be necessary to create a trademark registration in case of future patenting.

6.   Licences and Permits

There are varieties of business licences and permits that may apply to your particular situation, depending on the type of business you are starting, and location may also be an important consideration.

Licences and permits for professionals, e.g. Architects, Engineers, etc. Research directly or by engaging learned persons may be a viable way to go.

7.   Accounting System

An independent or chartered accountant can be engaged to set up a basic template for creation and management of budget, set-up rates and prices, an accounting manual and procedure in filing tax returns as and when due.

8.   Business Location

Setting up your place of conducting business is very important for the operation of your business; whether you have a home office, a shared or private office space or a retail location. The nature of your business will be very important in making this decision. You will need to consider the location, equipment and overall set-up, making sure the eventual location and access is ideal for your kind and type of business. Engage the services of an estate agent, if necessary.

9.   Work Team and Employees

A clear business plan will indicate the type of suitable personnel for your business, and you may need to engage the services of a management consultant with experience in human resources management to guide and advise or even to assist selection to engage.

Make sure the available positions are clearly outlined alongside job responsibilities that are part of each position.

You may also decide on the outsource options to other contractors, making sure that they will not turn out to be your competitors, and the arrangement between the parties should be clearly worked out by an experienced lawyer.

A 'solopreneur' could make do with a mentor, a business coach, your family for motivation, advice and reassurance. Whichever the option, do consider the following vital points in employee management and sustenance, i.e.

i.   A good communication with your team
ii.   Decision-making must drive inclusiveness
iii.   Empowerment freedom to a willing participation
iv.   Work-life balance to reduce over-burden
v.   Career planning and development for growth and sustainability
vi.   Reward and recognition.

10. Operations Start-up/Running

The success of a business largely depends on attracting the best clients and customers. There may be the need to engage a marketing firm for advice and guidance or even to propose a strategic approach to launching your business into the market place.

This is the time to utilise your previous resources of networking to create the business of your choice that works.

8

The making of a successful enterprise

Gi - 38

"Partnership and collaboration are essential in the long-term success of businesses"

———————

Muhammadu Indimi

———————

• • •

THE MAKING OF A SUCCESSFUL ENTERPRISE

Key Factors

Breathing life into an organisation goes beyond injecting funds to satisfy legal and social requirements. It begs sustainability to grow and continually be the most desired among competition. The leadership stoops and eventually rears its head only when the company's strength grows through conversion of weaknesses to strength and threats to opportunities. Knowing the scope and limits of the desired goal for a period goes a long way to focusing on achieving the desired outcome for climbing the ladder of performance.

Ensuring that the chain does not break means conscientious action with formidable coherence of all stakeholders for the desired success ranking.

Aspects of value to the enterprise can therefore be viewed in the following areas:

1. Vision
2. Mission
3. Policy
4. Objectives
5. Organisation (Director/Leader Manager who is focused, visionary, committed, strategy-laden, selfless, etc.), Structure, Function, Division of Labour

6.   Legal Status

7.   Corporate Management

8.   Finance

9.   Brand identity

10. Resource Management

11. Culture

12. Value

13. Corporate Responsibility

14. Collaboration

15. Communication Means, Barriers, Authority, Network and Openness.

1. Vision

Every enterprise sets out through a perceived futuristic view, the focal point of a perspective called vision. This usually starts with a person with a creative mind or an attracted set of people of similar interests for their own future and that of the wider community.

2. Mission

Following the vision, the next step is to set a mission: having identified and understood the opportunities and challenges, a solution is determined and established as the best fit for extending the opportunities and addressing the challenges for the beneficiaries, i.e. customers or clients in the long term. A statement that best captures this solution is then made so as to continually set and guide the company towards the focus of delivering the desired satisfaction.

3. Policy

Discipline is the best tool to achieving great results of any value; similarly, organisational policy is a list of the appropriate discipline pathway the enterprise must channel through for the best of the desired outcome. Therefore, the leadership first ensures that there is a statement of guiding policy for every aspect of the operation of the business, including for employees, machines, money, materials, market, etc.

This is vital, as it sets out the standards and drives the quality of the products and services as well as the returns on the invested resources at any period. The responsibility to develop the right policy most suitable for a desired strategically defined objective in a sustainable manner cannot be underestimated. Similarly, the need to review, amend, validate and add value to a policy structure of an enterprise at the end of each company year must be seen as beneficial.

An enterprise without a policy framework will have a tendency to attend to issues with the rule of thumb which does not connect and offers no continuity and portends a complex system that requires a new rule at every business event occurrence to address similar concern.

4. Objectives

This is a statement of clear facts without ambiguity on what the enterprise wishes to achieve on the matter or subject of its business. This statement is objective if only the object to realise is known and stated in the most appropriate unit that can be understood as aligning with the subject's product, goods, services or any item of unit that can be measured. Such objectives include: number of units of products, market share, revenue size, customer or client type or size, buying or leasing, etc., which cut across all sections or divisions of the enterprise.

This provides the indicators for measuring the growth rate of the business over a predetermined period. The objectives are usually based on previous performance with a view towards beating the existing record and improving overall performance.

5. The Organisation

The production of the products or services of the company requires a form of organisation and the process chart that are most suitable for optimal performance in operation, productivity, profitability and continuity. There is nothing like one organisation fits all businesses. It is the required production or service operations, depending on which is applicable to the enterprise that should inform the structure in place or to be adopted.

Every company desires a growth curve that keeps growing and never declines. This can only be achieved with the right and matching structure in place at every instance, such that the business owners recognise when the client demands outweighs the people's skills and time in the company, thus beckoning the injection of additional people with competence, ability and enthusiasm for production of offerings that provide client satisfaction. The unquestionable fact is that the vision is always larger than the founder, and so the more the enterprise expands the more the need for modification of the structure. Stemming from a micro-enterprise, delegation of tasks to employees will enable the owners to focus on jobs that only they can do, better permitting expansion of the company while competent employees are assigned to other necessary tasks.

The suitable structure will depend strongly on the size of the business. While small enterprises may be able to stand with a few employees and one or two managers assisting the owner, who performs the role of the overseer or Director, a large enterprise will require a more robust structure that includes a corporate governance function with appointed directors for managing the business for the benefit of the shareholders.

Fundamental Hierarchical Levels in a Medium Enterprise

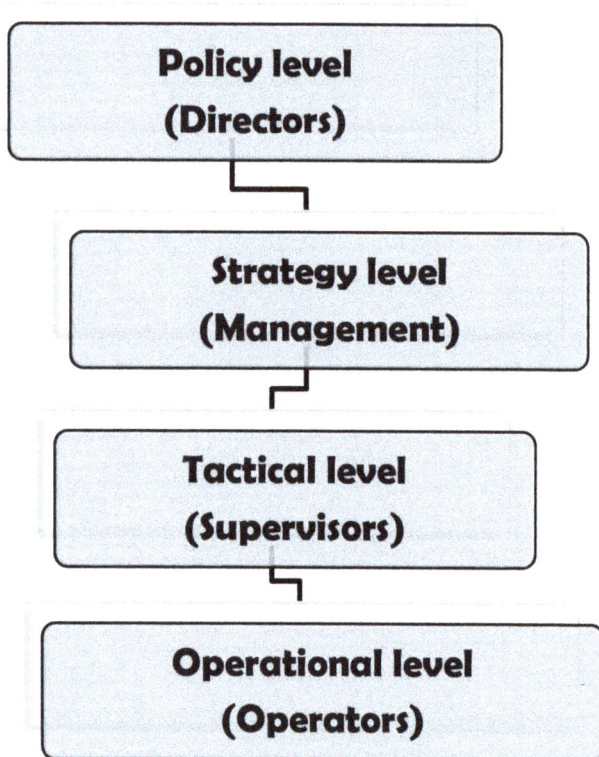

**Policy level
(Directors)**

**Strategy level
(Management)**

**Tactical level
(Supervisors)**

**Operational level
(Operators)**

Gi - 40

It was stated that, according to the Michigan Supreme Court (Friedman, 1998), "A business corporation is organised and carried on primarily for the profit of the stockholders. The powers of the directors are to be employed for that end. The discretion of directors is to be exercised in the choice of means to attain that end and does not extend to a change in the end itself, to the reduction of profit or to the non-distribution of profits among stockholders in order to devote them to other purposes."

The directors therefore have power to execute their tasks and take decisions in the following areas:

- Business expansion
- Territorial expansion
- Budget approval
- Profit/loss sharing to owners or payment of dividends to stockholders.

The directors likewise delegate roles to officers with authority to act on behalf of the organisation. The officers are employees of the company and are under the span of control of the directors.

6. Legal Status

An enterprise is a recognised legal entity that can sue and be sued. This requires that there are statutory requirements that the organisation must meet to be considered statutorily compliant and be off the arm of the law. This calls for a procedural approach, the size of the company notwithstanding. Usually, a competent legal secretary is engaged to address all that is required and to ensure that the company is well positioned as regards statutory integrity. A medium to large entity or a service provider entity may consider internalising its legal function if it deals on contract with regular diverse documentation of agreements with several clients. An example would be an enterprise that offers software as a service (SAAS), internet providers and multinationals, etc.

7. Corporate Management

Apart from agreements that require the services of the legal practitioner, there are other areas where compliance is required and it is the responsibility of the enterprise management or directors to ensure compliance and be off the arm of the law. These include: government taxes, insurance, pension, professional practice licences, employee nationalities and resident permits, rates and bills for services enjoyed directly or indirectly, etc.

It is therefore mandatory to know the necessary compliance that must be met as a corporate body in the domicile environment.

8. Finance

This is the lubricant of all parts of the enterprise. A well-designed finance policy, skilfully managed, with a deep sense of discipline by those entrusted with its implementation, can result in an unstoppable record of high-yielding returns.

Enterprise finance is deeply rooted in capital invested by its founders and subsequently from creditors, retained funds, loans, monetary instruments such as bankers' cheques, credit paper, government industry development loans, public share offerings, etc.

The key role of management is to achieve the maximum return on investment through human resources by satisfying customers. Therefore, identifying expected returns before a decision to add a new product line, investing in an asset or expanding into new areas are the best directors can ensure to avoid a sinking fund and performance decline in the unlikely event.

Subdivisions of the enterprise are responsible revenue or cost centres in either generating or incurring expenditure or both. This is of significant interest as the performance of each division must be closely and strictly monitored prudently to maintain proper liquidity for the enterprise at all times. Every enterprise must determine the best-fit strategy at a particular period towards a predetermined financial objective.

Gi - 41

Ensuring that the requirement of the financial regulatory authority of the host country or region is met in the most appropriate time keeps an enterprise in the good books of the authority, which will regard the company as a very responsible enterprise that meets its financial obligations to the government and its people where it operates. These regulations can be international, regional and local. All that is applicable must be identified and complied with, while keeping abreast of the frequent changes.

As part of planning, budgets are directed at specific targets and objectives from the various divisions if they exist, appraisal of which presents the evidence of performance and how realistic the budget was bearing in mind the competence of the budget promoters and the implementers.

To further ensure due process and ensure that employees strictly observe guidelines and procedures in their operations, internal audit becomes a veritable part of the functions within the company, while external audit consultants should be brought in at appropriate times to ascertain conformity.

9.   Brand Identity

Logo, signage, tagline, slogan and key titles: all these can be found or be part of an enterprise, but do they really completely depict the way it is perceived. Different target groups have different needs or wants and need to be considered and factored into your brand's outlook if you believe they matter to the final value of your company.

The overt view or opinion is not sufficient; the covert requires more attention than the overt. There are many ways a company can determine how it is perceived. Recently, online customer surveys through a feedback form are commonly used. Others organise a public awareness or information forum that attracts those who believe in their offerings and would be adopters. The responses from these give indication of the following of the company's brand in addition to its online presence. A strong brand will attract a large following, increase revenue and expand its customer size.

In essence, brand building must be regarded as a strong factor for promoting the continuity of the enterprise. The question will therefore be: what is your enterprise identity? How is the company perceived? What do you know about your company? What do people know about your company? How do people regard your company?

10. Resource Management

As agreed by several schools of thought, the resource components for viability through the perspective of a success-driven enterprise can be viewed as follows:

a. **Human being** — It is further stressed that the most important of all these is the human being, due to the general consensus that without being able to think, there would not be an idea to found any business or grow it from the foundation to an enviable competitive position.

- The human component is the most necessary resource without which no business can start or stand.
- The most sensitive resource for business
- Must be selected with a high level of discretion, focus and firmness.
- Selection decision offers no guarantee and therefore competent recruiters and internal assessment is advised.
- An amount of training is required for new employees to offer the desired outcome after being engaged. This is important to familiarise with the new environment physically and mentally.

- A suitable reward system will offer the newly engaged the opportunity to be internally motivated with a proper focus on the job for a reasonable period, so long as the offer is competitive within the industry. A motivating review will keep employee mobility low.

b. **Money** — As earlier discussed under finance, funding is the lubricant of an enterprise, and other resources are inactive without it. This makes it highly important to manage prudently for business continuity. The right decision today may be the wrong decision the very next day; when the market is volatile, it therefore takes a very dynamic, alert and pragmatic leader to handle the final decision on the issue of an enterprise fund management in order to ensure liquidity at all times and good yielding investments.

Gi - 42

c. **Market** — The clients or customers are domiciled in a particular territory of interest to the enterprise; this is the market. To this fact, there will be territorial concern for the business whether it operates locally, regionally or internationally, or in any combination. The needs and demands for the market must be met continually to remain significantly and profitably there.

Technology requirements differ, from local to international or widespread coverage. While moderately priced software for processing transactions of a moderate number served locally, software that provides virtual meetings or conferencing may be required for an international or regional company for effective real-time communication to match competition.

d. **Materials** — These may be sourced locally or from other countries. The requisite regulations must be known and applied conscientiously to avoid hitches in stock levels. An inventory must be planned and recorded as internal transactions towards final reports of accounts at the end of the accounting year. Locally sourced items must also be well documented to ensure that the records are available when needed. Records of suppliers are also kept; while some are creditors, others are cash-based. In line with Total Quality Management (TQM), materials should not be over-stocked to avoid expiration and reduce rejects. A well-managed material system from quality to price to inventory will minimise waste, increase production efficiency and yield higher return.

e. **Machinery** — From desktop computers to the operation control hand-held devices, the heavy loading and delivery equipment, tankers, cranes, cooling towers, rational cookers, millers, spectrometers, to mention a few diverse equipment, depending on each company's requirement, are the inevitable components of business. Each company's specific equipment, which is directly related to production of its products and services, is a significant investment for the company.

Machines must be maintained sustainably, be treated as having a lifecycle, with an appropriate maintenance system, while each is regarded as perpetual through a systematic provision of depreciation value for its replacement at the end of the cycle.

They are, however, never self-operating; no matter how automatic the design concept, a human operator is still essential. Technological advancement has in no mean measure reduced the number of personnel a company will require to operate these machines, due to their extensive in-built auto-control system.

It is the strategic responsibility of the management to determine and decide the appropriate type of machine and which specification most efficiently meets the desired objective for a specific goal.

f.   Management — This responsibility organises, controls and oversees the co-ordination of the affairs and operations of the enterprise, capturing all areas of need and ensuring that gaps are identified and effectively provided for. Hence, an enterprise deserves to have competent, experienced and committed employees with the right education, training, hard and soft skills, as well as being conversant with appropriate technology to match each area or division of the enterprise to be managed.

A manager must be a good communicator, a people's person, yet firm. He has to be a role model at work and an ambassador of the company anywhere else.

The management may be formed of more than one person, depending on the size of the enterprise. In a micro-scale business, for example, there may be one manager and management who decides, controls and communicates both with the employees internally and external contacts (government, suppliers, contractors, etc.).

As the enterprise grows in services or product offerings to a small-scale enterprise, the responsibility will also increase; and, as earlier mentioned, it soon becomes necessary to divide the tasks into specific target functions and employ others with the right competence to deliver the roles on the specific functions. This also applies in the case where there is expansion into other territories. The growth rate therefore determines the management size.

11. Culture

Each enterprise through the principles of its founder and the operating policies, internal culture is derived and employees easily belong and further mould and are identified by it. This is the organisational culture. It reflects significantly on how things are done and how employees relate with each other inside and outside the company. Leadership drives culture in an organisation with characteristics such as attitude, value, timeliness, attire, how grievances are resolved, and so on.

Culture as a factor attracts the right stakeholders to the company and a contributor to productivity.

Individual Development Guide for a Healthy Living:

A guide towards developing the right attitude for a successful business life

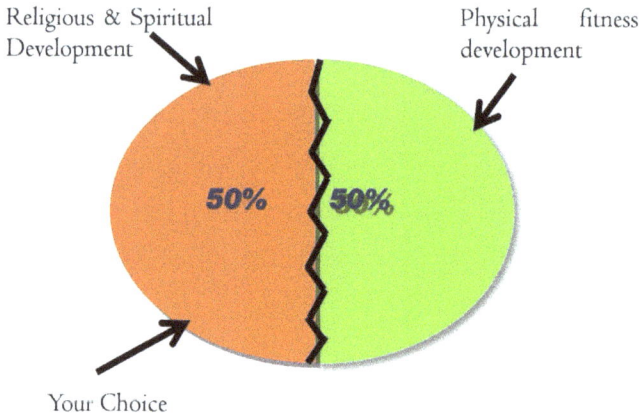

Religious & Spiritual Development

Physical fitness development

50% 50%

Your Choice

Golfing is all

- Requirement / desire
- Well being
- Networking & Socialization
- Ethics & Orientation
- Enhanced focus
- Leisure / Admiration /Prestige

Gi - 43

12. Value

Value can be regarded as the extent to which the product is appreciated by the customer; in other words, every customer expects a degree of value as reciprocal to the amount he pays in consideration. Therefore, the value has to be balanced or higher for the recipient to really appreciate the product.

For optimal appreciation, therefore, the customer/client and consumer must be at the centre of the decision that an enterprise makes, because each and every decision eventually leads to an action. It thus behoves the management to deploy strategic action to entrench the right attributes that will impact desired outcomes of efficiency, effectiveness, integrity and fairness along the value chain of the enterprise. This is what will be seen as the enterprise value.

The resultant effect will transcend along the supply chain to the extent of sending a wave of influence which the suppliers may adopt and replicate.

In addition, the reward of customer value perception can increase customer size and sales, boost revenue and profit and encourage company growth.

In the long run, the company goodwill token should be made to remain on the balance to maintain the growth curve. The token must keep increasing so the company acquires goodwill. The goodwill is directly proportional to the level of growth, so when the goodwill falls, the curve declines. The managers must ensure that the goodwill of the company is always maintained at its peak.

13. Corporate Responsibility

It is that which is obligatory to perform by the enterprise to the state or the government as a matter of policy of government in the environment where the company operates. It is necessary for the nature and extent of this obligation to be identified, determined and structured into the plan of the enterprise and be executed timely.

Usually, government sets up regulatory authorities for each of the requirements under this obligation, which may include the following list, among others:

- Building Location
- Building Design and Content
- Professional Practice Licence
- Procurement Standard (relevant categories)
- Corporate and Business Tax
- Financial Regulatory Standard
- Employee Compensation and Retirement Plan
- Health and Safety at Work
- Insurance (relevant categories)
- Corporate Governance (small-scale to large corporations)
- Company Annual Reports and Filings, etc.

These and many more are to be considered, depending on the country or state of domicile of the company. The Management must therefore be sensitive to the significance of meeting the obligation to the company's acceptance, goodwill and its brand's value in all its locations.

14. Collaboration

Why is this necessary?

Most business ideas may not be new anymore due to the influence of the dynamics of digital communication. The products or services that are the key offerings of your company here may be an offering of a subsidiary of another company in another part of the world that has achieved significant success and growth in it that may inspire others with determination to succeed in the business. It is therefore advisable to form a sort of inter-relationship alliance with such a company.

The benefits derivable from such an alliance or collaboration include:

- Knowledge transfer
- Mentoring, i.e. training of relevant personnel through suitable arrangements
- Specialty equipment and material sourcing
- Specialty professional recognition
- Multi-region and/or local professional recognition
- Powerful coverage and protection
- Stronger position in the operating environments
- Promotes trust and business relationships with financial institutions
- Attracts the best employees in the industry
- Improves overall company performance
- Promotes company growth and expansion

15. Communication

This is purely transmitting information to the desired recipient effectively and efficiently. The need to communicate widely and continuously is as important as the existence of the enterprise. All facets of the organisation should be linked in a network of communication, passing information across as soon as needed. This is further classified into two categories:

a. Internal communication

b. External communication.

What is common to both is the existence of an originator, a recipient, as well as the means through which the information flows, referred to as the channel of communication.

a. Internal communication

Direct communication through a face-to-face medium such as at meetings using verbal and written address at physical premises, often with a routine schedule, is still very common and is viewed as acceptable standard. More so in order for the company to attend to the day-to-day requirements as well as for strategic planning of operations and other relevant decision-making with input from identified teams.

Urgent information is usually transmitted by telephone calls or short messaging service (SMS) as well as by outlook network or electronic mail (Email). A company with several outlets with the digital system using enterprise resource planning (ERP) can have a network of the employees connected on the platform from many locations, communicating with each other over very long distances in a very short time. Similarly, the use of SKYPE for virtual meetings is adopted by companies with multiple locations. This type of communication creates an environment that eliminates the barrier of distance and time and lowers the turnaround time, with a cost-saving effect.

The importance of internal communication is to ensure that resources are deployed to meet the objectives of the period in focus, harnessing various functions for overall business performance.

Beyond the means is the interpretation of the message by the recipient. The originator must give clear, concise and simple information in the acceptable official language at all times to avoid misinterpretation and misapplication, giving no room for ambiguity.

Thus, the relationship between the originator and the recipient must be construed as that of internal customer. Due to the face-to-face nature, in many cases gestures and body language of the originator may either enhance or distort the interpretation by the recipient. Therefore, etiquette must form part of the consideration to promote positive gestures and the right body language.

b.   External communication

A wide array of stakeholders receive messages from every enterprise, commencing from the start-up stage with government officials for registration, partners if any, consultants, field experts, candidates, landlord, other billing authorities, bank, insurer(s); while suppliers and creditors as well as investors soon join the array.

The stakeholder that often comes to the fore is the client or customer in the target market. In as much as the customer matters, it is the consumer at the end of the chain that finally responds to the effect of the product, especially in a business-to-business (B2B) relationship. Hence, the consumer must be at the breath of the message for overall effectiveness. In addition, an enterprise communication is of great importance to competitors and even incoming entrants.

To ensure that information flows desirably and each stakeholder has the right information at the appropriate time, it is necessary to identify, plan and develop individual schedules with the six Ws.

For example:

Who — XYZ insurance company

Why — Annual insurance premium (recurring)

What — Professional indemnity, vehicle insurance, accident insurance, premises insurance, etc.

When — April every year

How — Telegraphic bank transfer

Where — Location address of the insurance company.

Similarly, tax office communication concerns remittances, while the company registrars' communication concerns filing of annual returns, and each communication schedule will be focused on each concern.

Notably, the fast pace at which digital technology enhances information delivery and marketing communication to the customers now spreads fast on the internet and across the social media. This bears a lot of advantage of wider coverage, faster reach, cost efficiency, online archive and many more.

16. Corporate Social Responsibility (CSR)

As a kind man may attract the kindness of his neighbours in times of need, so does an enterprise with strong goodwill in its business environment to attract the co-operation of its stakeholders.

Sensitivity to the social needs within its operating environment has been known to boost the acceptance of a company's products or services, e.g. most telephone and internet service providers often design products that address the needy as well as give back loyalty awards to their customers. Similarly, food companies use their marketing to offer scholarships to students for specific subjects or courses, while others dig boreholes and build schools for rural dwellers.

Several schools of thought have different opinions about how this should be carried out. While some believe that the enterprise must involve all relevant stakeholders in the decision of what is most desirable for the community so that the community can take ownership with active participation to maintain and sustain when projects are built for the community, others believe that philanthropy is sufficient, which is basically whatever the enterprise offers the community, and it is the responsibility of the community to derive benefit from it and optimise its value.

Gi - 45

Advertently, an enterprise will raise its own banner higher with an air of corporate social responsibility which often boosts the acceptability of the company as strategic sensibility among competition. It can further boost confidence, generate leads, new deals and strengthen goodwill that promotes company performance and growth through sustainability.

9

**Typical
template of
Business models**

"Attitude! Attitude!! Attitude!!!
Indisputable force for enhancing positive performance and
sustainability"

———————

Beatrice Alade

———————

A TYPICAL TEMPLATE OF BUSINESS MODEL FOR THE CREATIVE ENTREPRENEUR

1. Brief

Understanding the limits and delimits of a business is an essential ingredient for any business owner. This will guide the extent to which resources will be deployed to address each attainment or objective along the business formation and development. It therefore behoves on this presentation to elucidate common and uncommon areas for the benefit of the readers who shall hopefully find this a useful companion in the life of their businesses.

The clarity it provides can go a long way to assist an entrepreneur in managing communication with different professionals and agencies providing it with services. Furthermore, specific areas may be expanded beyond that which is presented, depending on the business environment and regulations where the business is established and/or operated.

2. Business Types

Business enterprises are categorised as follows, based on capacity and size of the business:

TYPE:	MICRO	SMALL	MEDIUM	LARGE
	■	■	■	■

The category usually for the purpose of comparison may apply capital base as the factor among other factors which may include customer volume, market share, number of employees, etc. The comparison must be of reference in the industry and market where the business operates.

3. Business Plan

Each business from commencement must have set out its plan of action towards the realisation of the business. This states all that is required for the start-up of the business through operation and likelihood of exit. It is the very essential and systematically developed foundation requirement prior to any start-up, tender for contracts, business expansion and when seeking grants for business.

Included in the plan are company registration, vision, mission, objectives, personnel, products, customers, market, location, finance, equipment, organisation, operating structure, revenue and expenditure forecasts, risks management strategy and exit strategy. This must appeal to all stakeholders that it is targeting or directed at. In other words, it must be convincing and clinch you the deal or the funding.

Depending on the industry in which the business will be operated, this plan should also serve as a guide to the managers of what the stakeholders would be expecting from them. Suffice it to say that all elements on the plan must be fed to the business as it incubates, to enable it to manifest positively, establish soundly and be sustainable.

4.   Finance Plan

Business needs to be fuelled with the requisite type and amount of funding to evolve, survive and be sustained. Whatever the size of the business, it needs access to capital, which comes with cost of capital. The owners must ensure that the concept of sustainability through prudency of financial management is condensed into corporate strategies and policies that ensure that funds flow to the appropriate beneficiaries, be it retained, invested or paid out to relevant stakeholders. It is therefore important to have strategies that deliver a competitive advantage in the industry to attract capital at cheaper cost.

Sole trader and sole professional consultants often invest their own capital to start up the business, in which case self-discipline must be at the top of the ladder to ensure that the fund is matched with strict prudency to avoid depletion while further growing the strength of the fund as necessary during the business life-cycle. Striking the right balance in entrepreneurial flair and minimising the risk of value destruction is fundamental to sustainable fund performance.

In a partnership, the business is funded according to the fraction of their ownership as agreed by all partners, and they share the profit and loss similarly, otherwise as statutorily permitted.

Ethical, social and environmental issues must be considered in all cases of fund access in order to protect the value of the business. A business with strong ethical, social and environmental values shows low risk to loan repayment and assets deposited as security, whereas high-risk land with environmental problems deposited as security, it will lead to higher borrowing charges.

5. Business Structure

It is important to identify under what structure the business will operate at the beginning, even though this may be changed as the business progresses, depending on the resources and capacity the intending owner is willing to deploy and whether he wants to start alone or partner with relevant others at the beginning.

Sole ownership rests the entire liability on a single owner, very common in a consultancy business, while partnership, a progressive option in a consultancy business, enables the diffusion of liabilities across several owners. Next is the limited liability structure, which limits the obligation to the business entity itself, except in cases where regulation may require the attention of the directors.

6. Business naming

A name is the first selling point for any business, just like for anyone. It is often believed that a name influences the character of a person; therefore, choosing the most appropriate name will require critical thinking and focus on the mission of the enterprise. If the mission is to provide comfort, then names that depict comfort are a best match. For example, 'Optima Creation', 'Sweet Home', etc., depending on the field of practice.

7. Licensing and Permits

Every business requires some sort of licensing from start-up to business development. A licence is a permit that authorises the business to operate in and from the community or territory in which it is located.

Recently, inclusion of virtual trade online and by telesales has further expanded the location of most companies globally; therefore, licensing may be required in other locations apart from where the physical business address is found. The rules and regulations vary from country to country and entrepreneurs must use this as an opportunity to learn and trade while interacting with other cultures and ideas around the globe.

While a business or a professional entrepreneur needs to be licensed by a recognised professional body before it can operate and be professionally recognised, this must be taken seriously, as it is what assists the professional entrepreneur to climb the ladder and increase his share of the business in the industry with time, thus growing the business.

A permit, on the other hand, may not have professional restrictions, as this applies to ownership or partial ownership of assets in a business. In some cases, a business may require a permit to transact business with third parties on behalf of the client, thus serving as an agent to the client. This depends on the industry of the business.

It is therefore necessary for every entrepreneur to determine what aspect of the business will require a licence or permit in order to prevent possible litigation.

8.   Accounting System

If the business is not an accounting practice, then getting an accountant or a book-keeper (for micro-business) is inevitable. This is to ensure that all monetary transactions are well recorded for various reporting needs. Reports which include cash-flow statement, income statement, statement of financial positions, rate of returns, etc., using the appropriate financial policies and procedures in place and in accordance with the target stakeholder(s), must be purpose-driven and hold clarity for understanding by the stakeholder(s).

9.   Location

The choice of location must be derived from the target customer the business is to serve. This is commercial practice. Effort should be geared towards ensuring that the business reaches most of its target customers with minimal cost, whereby it locates in places where the customer can reach and comfortably transact business with it, except in the case of a fully online business. Therefore, for high-end customers, location within a metropolis in a city will be more ideal than locating downtown. Similarly, a midday food caterer or supermarket will be better close to the commercial centre of a city for heavy footfall daily.

In all cases, location must be reachable, appealing and secured to the target customer or client and be cost effective or, better still, a realistic cost for the business.

10. Employees

This is determined by the level of the business, at start-up. A sole entrepreneur may be the only employee, especially in consultancy, while he outsources other responsibilities to external providers. The demand for more internally engaged employees must be based on an increase in demand generated by the business. The higher the demand for the products and/or services of the business, the larger the employees may become, though not necessarily in proportional order, due to the possibility to optimise the capacity that already exists and may be under-utilised. Hence, an attempt to maximise capacity utilisation must be a priority at all times for value generation.

Persons with the right skills, duly certified qualifications and requisite experience in the field sought should be engaged and not the contrary. This will ensure that the job is appropriately delegated to whom can easily be further developed to assume higher roles whenever that becomes necessary.

The employer should ensure that the employee is well motivated at all times to deliver on the engagement promise which must have been agreed from the outset. In this case, the employer thinks ahead of the employee using the employment policy of the company, which must always be referred to at different times to honour its obligation to the staff.

11. Reward Management

This must be properly matched to the nature of the job of each employee, whereby piece-rate, time-rate or fixed-rate reward systems or a combination may be the best match for a particular job type than another. This will ensure that the employee focuses on how to best deliver his tasks efficiently with no labour overpay.

12. Performance Appraisal

Routine appraisal must be established to determine the performance of each member of staff over a reasonable period. A self-appraisal platform can be created on an internal portal for individual entry of one's own perception of self-performance at the end of the day, week or month. Management may thereafter undertake a staff appraisal from a management angle to summarise the actual performance per staff. This can be used to determine those who are outstanding, strong or weak on the job. The outstanding may be considered for higher responsibilities such as a supervisory role if available; the strong are best fit for the job; while the weak need more assistance or training to deliver on the job.

However, counselling and a change of task may also be found helpful with a weak employee.

13. Marketing/Launching/Promotion

Marketing is a means for any business to communicate the offering to target customers or clients in the most appropriate manner, using the right medium for effectiveness.

Your goods or service must have started with an idea/concept development to design development through customer testing or client approval.

First is to determine what type of marketing your product requires. What marketing organisation can give you the best package? Do you require internal tools, materials, equipment, skilled employees for this purpose, and how many? What do you really require for a true marketing success?

Product launch is usually a marketing campaign. Goods and services will follow different patterns of product launch, because one is tangible and the other may not be tangible until other inputs are added to it or it is delivered. The approach for a goods launch will consider the following:

- Know your target market.
- Know the target customers within the target market.
- Identify how best to reach and communicate (what channels

or media) your product offering to the target customers.

- Produce a specific product launch package size as souvenirs.
- Ensure that you predetermine demand (through a previous product testing and market testing exercise and customer survey report), produce and stock minimum estimated quantities of finished goods that will be reasonable enough for an instant order.
- Ensure that you establish the availability of enough materials (about 200% sold at product launch) for subsequent demand.
- Organise the product launch event at a venue and time most attractive to the target customers.
- Arrange all requirements for the event.
- Invite key stakeholders.
- If launched in a classy location indoors, follow-up to a wider audience through an outdoor campaign if desired.
- Do a customer feedback survey to know what they like most and what they still desire to receive.
- Do an appraisal of the campaign thereafter and watch the growth of the demand in sales and profit.
- Then establish a continuous process to always appraise, evaluate, assess, apply necessary modification and re-launch.

To promote your product is to learn to do more and give more to also receive more from all stakeholders. Promotional items can help put the product in customers' view throughout a business day and even at home. Items like mugs, key-holders, notepads, biros, wristbands, caps, towels, day planners, etc., are known to be on the attractive side and probably found useful by medium- to high-end customers. These well-branded items are reminders and may also provide relevant information for mouth-to-mouth promotion of the product by the holder.

You may also find it convenient to purchase an online marketing application, e.g. on Google. For uploading information and pictures about your product to a wide range of prospective customers, use social media such as Facebook, Instagram, Pinterest, etc., to show your products to followers; and online search as well as upload your products as part of the content on your website. In addition, you may subscribe for search-engine optimisation (SEO) to get priority listing of your product when prospects are searching online.

Service as a product will benefit greatly from marketing through online listing, website content management and SEO, in addition to various promotional hallways.

BUSINESS TEMPLATES FOR THE CREATIVE INDUSTRY

This aims at bringing an insight into what certain professionals in the creative industry should expect as the fundamentals of practice at different levels of the business set-up.

Firstly, a look at micro-business set-up by an individual who has acquired the requisite education and professional training and perhaps has also worked in a relevant organisation as an employee and desires to go into his own practice. To delve into entrepreneurship, taking the responsibility to own a business of this nature must require the basic necessity to hit the ground running.

Thus the starting point will be to list out what is required as follows for micro, small, medium or large enterprises, depending on what level the starting point is.

1.   Micro-Business Enterprise

This can be considered to be a sole trader category whereby the business is run by its registered owner. Table I below shows the essential components required for this business type, among others.

2.   Small-Business Enterprise

The next step is for a Small Enterprise, whereby the sole owner of a micro-business has seen the potential to grow into a larger company, the management of which goes beyond the capacity of one man. This can be as a result of increasing demand for the same offering or for added offerings in different areas of capability or professionalism beyond the strength of the owner and sole business. This calls for expansion into wider areas of the business to accommodate new intakes as co-investors and/or direct employees. The details in the table below will position the enterprise in the right order.

The company now moves to become a registered company, which may be a limited liability company, shortened as Ltd for the purpose of reporting and other statutory compliance.

3. Medium-Business Enterprise

Upward growth from Small Enterprise leads to Medium Enterprise, whereby the policy focus will be more stringent and the objectives will be determined by the next success level that the company wishes to achieve.

All the requirements in the small enterprise must have been met exhaustively, with enough preparedness to move forward into a larger operational and investment demand. The additional areas for policy change are indicated in Table I. Note that the business must be experiencing positive growth in selected rates of return (ROR) indicators to inform the management or shareholders of the need to expand into this level of business reinvestment, as well as the possibility to invite new relevant investors or partners.

Business Template for Different Enterprise Levels *Table 1*

COMPONENT	ENTERPRISE LEVEL			
	MICRO	SMALL	MEDIUM	LARGE
Business owner	√			
Registered Company Name	√			
Registered Company	√	√	√	√
Registered Directors		√	√	√
Registered Subscribers/Owners	√	√	√	√
Registered Shareholders		√	√	√
Registered Company Secretary		√	√	√
Registered Location	√	√	√	√
Finance	√	√	√	√
Office Space	√	√	√	√
Banking	√	√	√	√
Equipment: Industry-specific equipment and tools	√	√	√	√
Office Management equipment and consumable	√	√	√	√

Table 1 continued

COMPONENT	ENTERPRISE LEVEL			
	MICRO	SMALL	MEDIUM	LARGE
Personnel Recruitment: Industry-certified Manpower	√	√	√	√
Essential Labour (permanent, term, casual, freelance, etc.)	√	√	√	√
Consultants	√	√	√	√
Contractors		√	√	√
Continuous Development	√	√	√	√
Reward Management	√	√	√	√
Intellectual (Creative) Property Protection; Trademark	√	√	√	√
Copyright	√	√	√	√
Information Management System (IMS); Strategic Management hardware	√	√	√	√

Table 1 continued

COMPONENT	ENTERPRISE LEVEL			
	MICRO	**SMALL**	**MEDIUM**	**LARGE**
Strategic Management software	√	√	√	√
IMS Training	√	√	√	√
Communication; Website	√	√	√	√
Email	√	√	√	√
Telephone	√	√	√	√
Radio	√	√	√	√
Networks (social/ professional media, etc.)	√	√	√	√
Digital Business Management; Industry-specific software	√	√	√	√
Industry-specific training	√	√	√	√
Company Accounting; Accounting		√	√	√
Auditing; Internal Auditor		√	√	√

Table 1 continued

COMPONENT	ENTERPRISE LEVEL			
	MICRO	**MICRO**	**MICRO**	**MICRO**
External Auditor		√	√	√
Taxation	√	√	√	√
Commercial; Marketing	√	√	√	√
Regional Marketing			√	√
International Marketing				√
Online Marketing	√	√	√	√
Advertising (may be restricted)	√	√	√	√
Networking	√	√	√	√
Sales; Business-to-Customer (B2C)	√	√		
Business-to-Business (B2B)		√	√	√
Business Expansion; Internal — Organic growth		√	√	√

COMPONENT	ENTERPRISE LEVEL			
	MICRO	SMALL	MEDIUM	LARGE
External — New products or new services		√	√	√
Location Expansion; Local Expansion		√	√	√
Regional Expansion			√	√
International Expansion				√
Corporate Management; Statutory Compliance	√	√	√	√
Security; Fund Protection	√	√	√	√
Asset Protection	√	√	√	√
Personnel Protection	√	√	√	√
Insurance; Professional Indemnity	√	√	√	√

Table 1 continued

COMPONENT	ENTERPRISE LEVEL			
	MICRO	SMALL	MEDIUM	LARGE
Group Personal Accident (GPA) Insurance		√	√	√
Premises Insurance	√	√	√	√
Asset insurance (Various risks)	√	√	√	√
Insurance Broker	√	√	√	√
Collaboration or Partnership		√	√	√
Research and Development	√		√	√
Corporate Governance			√	√
Legal Adviser	√	√	√	√
Stock Exchange Listing				√
Shareholders' Forum				√
Stock Broker				√

4. Large Business Enterprise

Further growth on the success of the Medium-Scale Business may require inviting the public to invest in the business. The business will transform into a Large Enterprise and become a Public Liability Company (PLC). This company will have met all the requirements of a medium enterprise and surpassed it by its capital layout, its internal capacity and external (market) acceptance.

The expansion can be achieved without international expansion if that is not statutorily required in the country of origin of the business. The enterprise may be referred to as a corporation, which requires policy change and additional structure to enhance its capability to deliver at that level, as shown in Table I above. This is the highest level and expansion can take any dimension, with diversification into other areas of diverse market demands in a more receptive global market.

GENERAL DEFINITIONS

Business Model

Business model is the actual existential structure of a business and represents the core aspect of the business in its operational existence. Business model is value driven as the enterprise attracts, converts, creates and delivers value to its target customers to generate and capture value combining economic, social and cultural contexts. The construction and modification of business model is part of an enterprise's business strategy. It will describe how customer value is delivered, paid for and profit realised.

An enterprise can navigate through business model innovation as the business grows by adding value expanding with new business model, diversification or acquiring new business model.

The importance of business model is useful to entrepreneurs, especially as the accounting standard bodies have incorporated them into the accounting standards for assets calculation and financial instruments classification. For example, for a manufacturing model, asset calculation may follow amortisation cost while for a retail model fair value cost may be followed in the asset calculation.

Among various types of business below are four business models that most enterprises fall into:

1. Manufacturer Business Model

The manufacturer business model considers that raw materials and/ or pre-fabricated components are combined to create a new product (e.g. cosmetics, plastic products, paints, etc.), or assembled into a product (e.g automobile, furniture, computers, mobile phones, etc.). In this model, the business sells its products or finished goods directly to its customers or outsourced seller companies, as part of its strategy. Examples are, Dangote Cement, Berger Paints, Royal Mills, Automobile Peugeot and PepsiCo.

2. Distributor Business Model

Distributor business model refers to those enterprises that purchase finished goods products directly from manufacturers for the purpose of resale. These products are sold to retail outlets or directly to individual customers. A notable example is a car distributor that purchases vehicles from the manufacturer and sells to customers that include businesses and individuals. Examples are, Coscharis Motors and Elizade Motors and Nortex Business Link.

3. Retailer Business Model

In retailer business model, products are purchased from a distributor for the purpose of resale directly to, individual customer or consumer. Historically, the brick and mortar shops signify the retailer. Nowadays, retail is synonymous with shopping malls and shopping centres (e.g. Park and Shop, Shoprite and Sahad Stores) while some enterprises using retail model can be found in local markets. Retail model is also exhibited by online retailers such as Amazon, Konga, Ali Baba, Kalahari, and Jumia to mention a few. Some retailers also combine online selling with their physical retail outlet sales, (e.g. Boots, Tesco, Dollar Pharmacy, American Golf Shop, etc.)

4. Franchise Business Model

In a franchise business model, the enterprise, a franchisee holds a license, which permits the execution of business with the identity of the Franchisor (the owner of the business identity). The franchisee usually pays a lump sum amount to the franchisor, as advance payment, towards royalty paid as a percentage of sales proceed or as described in the agreement. The license permits the holder to operate, as manufacturer, distributor or retailer, depending on type of business model purchased with the franchise. Commonly, the franchisor provides the franchisee technical, marketing and centralised administrative supports as well as requisite training. Examples are, Ariston, KFC, Eazi-Apps, Tantalizers and Recognition Express.

In addition to the four types of business models described above, an enterprise can structure its business model in more various ways:

- By direct dealing with customers, via the internet without any middleman.
- By product demonstration in prospective customer's home to sell directly to consumers, examples include: dealers in cosmetics, jewellery, health cookware, etc.
- By integrating physical and an online presence whereby customers can order online and receive goods delivered to them at a customer service centre or a store nearest to them.
- By using premium business model where the web service or product is offered for free, as basic, for a specified period

of time, while a premium has to be paid to use the special and advanced features
-   Another business model is holding an online auction over the internet.

5.   Typical Template

Refer to Table I.

6.   The Arts Gallery

Art gallery is the place where works of arts and crafts are stored for sale by either an entrepreneur or a hired gallery keeper. Creativity in arts brings out the expression of ideas, emotion or general views, which are communicated to people for information or aesthetic purposes. The various branches of creative arts commonly found in the art gallery include: painting, sculpture (wood, metal, stone, glass etc.), textile prints, leather works, collage, etc. Economic and social backgrounds are usually reflected in artworks as cultural component. Artworks generally hold the innate values in most cultures that transverse space and time. Arts can be viewed as a dynamic process of information which roles continually change overtime, with lower cultural roles and is presented as more of an aesthetic component in the market place. The art gallery in some countries may also offer the socio-educational function as a service to institutions of learning and even foreign embassies in their locations.

Other areas of arts which creative works or recordings may be found in the art gallery include music, dance, literature, and drama.

7. The Film Production

Film production here refers to movie that is produced for theatrical exhibition. Production is the process of making the film and refers to the various tasks that must be individually completely executed during the shooting of the film, which equally applies to photography, television, digital video productions. There are essentially three production stages namely: pre-production, production and post-production. Among the pre-production tasks are: location selection, cast selection, scenes set-up and management, raw footage capture, and usage of set designs, to name a few of the many pre-production tasks. Production is the second step in film creation where the acting proper takes place following the pre-production phase and finally the post-production stage with opportunities for film promotion, ticket sales etc.

Film production offer several tasks that serve as business opportunities for entrepreneurs. Many of these tasks are outsourced to companies and individual entrepreneurs by big film producers.

8. The Architect's Practice Studio

Refer to the book "Architecture as a Business" by Bello M..

Conclusion

Gi - 49

"Sustainable wealth creation through entrepreneurship is no doubt an impetus for growth of business and growth of economy"

John Alabi

CONCLUSION

This book has defined the creative industries as those industries manned by persons with creative assets, the A–Z of entrepreneurship and how to unlock all the potentials that lie therein, whilst still protecting and preserving the individual intellectual property.

The book has shown in clear terms how entrepreneurship training and knowledge is a must for all individuals and more from the creative persons and industries. The A–Z of entrepreneurship now provides a fair knowledge and the right pathway to enable creative persons to succeed in their various fields of endeavour by providing a broad spectrum approach to understanding what confronts them and how to deal with/manage the circumstances towards a right and positive development of a profitable venture.

The book is to be seen and taken as a reference guide, a text book and a personal companion for a successful entrepreneurial journey of life.

Finally, what is clearly obvious is that, entrepreneurship is the best contributor to a nation's economic development.

In order to have free or open market competition, like with democracy, it is fundamental to promote brand building and growth development. Free or open market theory's expression implies free competition, differentiation of uniqueness, brand distinction and individuality which culminate into real and tangible value additions.

A brand is of distinct personality (remember enterprise as an entity) and a product offer with a name. A brand personifies value, offering certainty in its uniqueness; the necessity for brands is value, while value is about worth and cost satisfaction and utility.

Every value offering is identified by definite unique features which include product name, the enterprise's corporate identity logo presented as symbol or sign, value proposition or promise, unique selling point, positioning statement, all depicting its personality profile.

The above features are essential in the creative planning and execution of the development of a brand for an enterprise. Every brand requires recognition and acceptance of its products in the operating market as a part of the process to build a brand. Every brand needs to maintain uniqueness, and enterprises make lots of effort to sustain brands and the uniqueness.

A strong brand can also provide a platform for re-engineering of other brands for mutual benefits especially in co-competition.

Self-employed persons, i.e. entrepreneurs are known to add tremendous value to the economic development of their nations and upward economic transformation. Notable among these are: Richard Branson and Aliko Dangote.

Every nation must focus and strongly give entrepreneurship practice its rightful place in the affairs of the nation, to keep it a productive and happy nation. Governments must provide the enabling environment and appropriate regulatory frameworks to ease business development and operations, rather than being a large employer of labour, and competing with private enterprises.

Therefore, business environment must be right and conducive, to enable the massive emergence of entrepreneurs, with businesses that promptly attract investors and thriving commerce, for building a healthy economy and happy nation.

I hope that the book remains beneficial in wealth creation and has indeed unlocked insights into the entrepreneurial potentials of the creative persons and the industries, as well as others who can put their knowledge and skills to good use for their own benefit and the society.

Thank you, and wishing all the creative entrepreneurs the best of luck and successes in their endeavours.

Gi - 50

Thank you, and best of luck in your endeavours

Entrepreneurship
Wisdom Titbits

"We are living in the age of the entrepreneur. The only major things it takes is the mind-set and right attitude."

Welcome to the world of micropreneur   Daniel Ochi

"One of the best messages I have gottttt...

Take chances... Tell the truth... Learn to say NO... Spend money on the things you love... Laugh till your stomach hurts... Dance even if you are too bad at it... Pose stupidly for photos... Be Child-like... Moral: Death is not the greatest loss in life... Loss is when life dies inside you while you are alive...

Celebrate this event called LIFE."

Awe post by MeMe

Why Mentor?

Mentoring, at its core, guarantees young people that there is someone who cares about them, assures them they are not alone in dealing with day-to-day challenges, and makes them feel like they matter. Research confirms that quality mentoring relationships have powerful positive effects on young people in a variety of personal, academic, and professional situations. Ultimately, mentoring connects a young person to personal growth and development, and social and economic opportunity. Yet one in three young people will grow up without this critical asset."

"One of the greatest values of mentors is the ability to see ahead what others cannot see and to help them navigate a course to their destination."

John C. Maxwell

"Push your Mentee.

As Henry Ford is reputed to have said, if you always do what you've always done, you will always get what you've always got. Learning requires stretching the mind and taking risks, says Zachary. A mentor facilitates this process by asking probing questions that challenge thinking.

Gross agrees: 'you need to get to the edge in order to grow,' he says. If you stay in the comfort zone all the time, that's where you'll be."

The Value of Mentoring *by Joelle Klein*

-Community- Mentor or be mentored. Either way, you gain valuable wisdom and experience – and a meaningful personal connection. The best thing about mentoring? There's something in it for everyone."

The Magic of Mentoring *by Karen Olson*

• • •
181

"Most of us can point to an influential person (or maybe several people) who has helped shape who we are today. These mentors have worked behind the scenes with us, generously sharing their time, expertise, and insights to nurture our potential, keep us on track, and help us grow — often personally and professionally.

'Mentors are wisdom keepers,' says Rabbi Victor Gross, co-director with his wife, Rabbi Nadya Gross, of the ALEPH Sage-ing Mentoring, a spiritual mentoring program in Boulder, Colo. What is wisdom? It's the combination of knowledge and experience."

The Value of Mentoring, by Joelle Klein

"The first secret: Attitude

Being successful in anything is largely about your attitude. Having a successful organisation is about having the right set of attitudes. These attitudes guide you in the key decisions of your business. They keep you going when times are tough. They are the difference between those who fail and those who succeed. Your attitudes are what your customers will pick up subconsciously and use in their decision to buy from you and buy from you again. Your attitude will be the difference between starting a business and starting a successful business."

How to be an entrepreneur, *by Steve Parks*

Other Books Recommended for Reading

1. *Architecture as a Business*, by Bello M.
2. *Architecture and National Development; Focus: Adaptation in Recession*, by Bello M.
3. *Rich Dad Poor Dad*, by Robert Kiyosaki

Global Opportunities for Young African Entrepreneurs

1. Institute for Canadian Citizenship (ICC) Fellowship for Young Leaders
2. Atlas Corps Fellowship for Emerging Global Leaders
3. Power Africa's Young Women in African Power Leadership Residential Training Program
4. DAAD Scholarships for Development-Related Postgraduate Courses
5. NOW-Us! (Nothing about us Without Us) Award (win up to €25,000 and a trip to the Netherlands)
6. The Global Study Awards (up to £10,000)
7. WARC Travel Grant for West African Postgraduate Scholars and Researchers
8. OFID Development Leaders Scholarship to attend One Young World Summit in the Hague
9. GSMA Mobile for Humanitarian Innovation Fund
10. LEAP Africa Social Innovators Programme and Awards (SIPA) for Social Entrepreneurs
11. 18th International Anti-Corruption Conference (IACC) Young Journalists Initiative (Fully-funded to Denmark)
12. CcHUB Media Fellowship for Storytellers
13. African Climate Change and Environmental Reporting (ACCER) Awards (Fully-funded to COP24 + $1000)
14. OWSD-Elsevier Foundation Awards for Early-Career Women Scientists (win $5,000 and a trip to USA)

15. Woodrow Wilson International Center Fellowship Program
16. coLABS Impact Investing Fund for Early-stage Social Enterprises
17. TechCrunch Startup Battlefield Africa (win US $25,000 and a trip to San Francisco)
18. Fair Play Competition for Young Bands (win a trip to Denmark for International Anti-corruption Conference)
19. Short Story Day Africa Prize for African Writers
20. ABEM Biomedical Engineering Scholarships for African Postgraduate Students & Academics
21. MEST/Merck Accelerator Lagos Satellite Program for Startups in West Africa (up to $3,000)
22. Accenture HealthTech Innovation Challenge
23. Emerging African Innovation Leaders G7 Exchange & Empowerment Program (Fully-funded to Milan, Italy)
24. Youth@IGF Program for the Internet Governance Forum in Paris, France
25. Mexican Government Scholarships for International Students
26. Merck Accelerator Cape Town Satellite Program for Start-ups in Southern Africa ($3,000 prize)
27. Leaders for Health Equity Fellowship Program
28. The Global Teacher Prize 2019 (US $1 million Award)
29. The Saville Foundation Pan-African Awards for Entrepreneurship in Education (win US $15,000)
30. The Platform Nigeria Young Professionals Bootcamp.
31. WorldLabs Elevating Ideas Competition (win £50,000 and a trip to Elevating Ideas London)

32. International Society for the Performing Arts (ISPA) Global Fellowship Program
33. APSA Challenge Science and Technology — Ethiopia for Young African Scientists and Entrepreneurs
34. UNESCO/Keizo Obuchi Research Fellowships
35. Girl Rising Creative Challenge (up to $2,000)
36. World Water Challenge — An International Contest for Water Solutions
37. Cartier Women's Initiative Awards for Entrepreneurs
38. Youth Peace Initiative Next Generation Peacebuilders Video Contest (win the Youth Carnegie Peace Prize)
39. World Bank Young Professionals Program
40. United Nations Young Professionals Programme
41. Jack Ma's Netpreneur $10 million prize for innovative entrepreneurs and start-ups in Africa

Some Professional Bodies in the Creative Sector in Nigeria

1. Advertising Practitioners Council of Nigeria
2. Association of Music Artistes Managers of Nigeria
3. Association of Movie Producers - Nigeria
4. Brand Journalists' Association of Nigeria
5. Chartered Institute of Marketing of Nigeria
6. Computer Association of Nigeria
7. Fashion Designers Association of Nigeria
8. Graphic and Web Design Association Of Nigeria
9. Institute of Software Practitioners of Nigeria
10. Institute of Chartered Accountants of Nigeria
11. Interior Designers Association of Nigeria
12. Nigeria Computer Society
13. Nigerian Institute of Architects
14. Nigerian Institute of Public Relations
15. Nigerian Publishers Association
16. Nigerian Society of Artists
17. Outdoor Advertising Association of Nigeria
18. The Musical Society of Nigeria
19. The Society for the Performing Arts in Nigeria

List of Illustrations, Pictures and Tables

Image number	Description	Source
Book Cover	Creative Industries	Image courtesy: https://www.lseg.com/resources/1000-companies-inspire-britain/creative-industries-0
Gi-01	Creative, talented, gifted	Image courtesy: http://iamjekker.com/blog/2269
Gi-02	Africa's creative industries sees unprecedented growth — the website for African entrepreneurs	Image courtesy: http://enterprise54.com/africas-creative-industries-sees-unprecedented-growth/
Gi-03	Concept of creative business with businessman working with laptop	Image courtesy: https://www.dreamstime.com/stock-image-creative-business-concept-businessman-working-laptop-image35888471
Gi-04	How the Nigerian creative industry can create wealth	Image courtesy: http://www.qdancecenter.com/single-post/2015/04/19/how-the-nigerian-creative-industry-can-create-wealth
Gi-05a	Creative industries summer showcase	Image courtesy: https://blogs.susu.org/blog/2015/05/29/creative-industries-summer-showcase/

Image number	Description	Source
Gi-05b	Spotlight on creative industries	**Image courtesy:** https://www.careerswales.com/en/spotlight-on-creative-industries/
Gi-06	Commentary on the creative industry in Kenya	**Image courtesy:** http://www.kreativekenya.co.ke/commentary-on-the-creative-industry-in-kenya/
Gi-07		**Image courtesy:** https://www.britcham.org.sg/static-pages/at-a-glance-creative-media
Gi-08	The overlapping nature of the Creative Industries and their Sectors	**Image courtesy:** Illustration by Farida Bello
Gi-09	Advertising campaign guide: a step-by-step procedure	**Image courtesy:** http://touchstonelimited.com/category/advertising/
Gi-10	The ins and outs of advertising	**Image courtesy:** https://www.bossimage.ca/ins-outs-advertising/
Gi-11	Watercolour sketch	**Image courtesy:** https://www.pinterest.com/alejandrovaldiv/arch-sketch-drawing/?lp=true

Image number	Description	Source
Gi-12	Art is an essential subject for children at school (corrected essay)	Image courtesy: https://ieltsonlinetests.com/writing-correction/art-essential-subject-children-school-corrected-essay
Gi-13	Celebrating 30 years: Developing people, ideas and opportunities through contemporary craft	Image courtesy: http://craftspace.co.uk/
Gi-14	Career opportunities for arts graduates in Nigeria	Image courtesy: Saci-florence https://ngcareers.com/course/436/arts
Gi-15	Immaculate designs — pearl white media graphic design services	Image courtesy: http://www.pearlwhitemedia.com/immaculate-designs-pearl-white-media-graphic-design-services
Gi-16	Rongrong illustration	Image courtesy: http://www.rongrongdevoe.com/
Gi-17	Movie film reel clipart	Image courtesy: http://pluspng.com/film-reel-png-3646.html
Gi-18	Music	Image courtesy: https://www.tss.qld.edu.au/prep-music-and-speech-amp-drama-may17/

Image number	Description	Source
Gi-19	Performing arts	Image courtesy: http://www. performingartsschoolgalway. com/
Gi-20		Image courtesy: https://hub. jhu.edu/magazine/2013/fall/ future-of-academic-publishing/
Gi-21	PC software	Image courtesy: http://www. webworkhouse.com/services/ technological-expertise/
Gi-22	Sha: TV & Radio	Image courtesy: http://www.sh-advertising.co.uk/ourwork. aspx?ow=110&typeId=14
Gi-23	Characteristics of Entrepreneurship	Image courtesy: http:// www.qsstudy.com/business-studies/characteristics-of-entrepreneurship
Gi-24	6+6 Drivers for Entrepreneurship	Image courtesy: http:// www.kotelnikov.biz/coach/ entrepreneur_12drivers.html
Gi-25	The One Thing An Entrepreneur Is More Than Anything Else	Image courtesy: http:// thematrixmastermind.com/one-thing-entrepreneur-more-than-anything-else/

Image number	Description	Source
Gi-26	The Entrepreneur	Image courtesy: Illustration by M.B. Bello
Gi-27	Creative Entrepreneurs	Image courtesy: http:// wecreate.global/creative-entrepreneurs/
Gi-28	The Creative Entrepreneur A-Z	Image courtesy: Table by M.B. Bello
Gi-29	Setting Up a Business Enterprise	Image courtesy: https:// www.slideshare.net/ amanpreetbhamra/setting-business-enterprise
Gi-30	Benefits Of Online Accounting	Image courtesy: https:// www.merrchant.com/ accountingsoftware/online-accounting-solutions/
Gi-31	Six Best Ways To Pursue Financial Goals	Image courtesy: https:// artofthinkingsmart.com/six-ways-to-pursue-financial-goals/
Gi-32		Image courtesy: http://www. gfjamesplumbing.com.au/blog/ pipe-relining-articles/how-pipe-relining-helps-save-cost-in-plumbing-repair
Gi-33	Cash Flow Management	Image courtesy: http:// events.r20.constantcontact. com/register/ event?oeidk=a07eeysku8x 2f908954&llr=zsoktncab

Image number	Description	Source
GI-34	Reporting line and span of control in an Accounting Department	Image courtesy: Illustration by Farida Bello
Gi-35	Managing Your Investment Risk By Understanding Your Risk Profile	Image courtesy: http://www.smartinvestor.com.my/managing-investment-risk/
Gi-36		Image courtesy: http://pkworldfree4u.blogspot.com/2014/03/idea-new-3g-udp-based-trick-working.html
Gi-37	Strategy – A good strong "why" will stop the arguments!	Image courtesy: https://gregcantyfuzion.com/2018/06/12/strategy-a-good-strong-why-will-stop-the-arguments/
Gi-38		Image courtesy: http://www.leadershub.org/motivation/23-keys-to-success-in-life/
Gi-39		Image courtesy: https://www.thehindubusinessline.com/specials/new-manager/designing-organisations-as-selfless-collectives/article7673895.ece
Gi-40		Image courtesy: Table by Farida Bello

Image number	Description	Source
Gi-41	Alternative Investments in Finance	Image courtesy: http://poitiers-finance.com/alternative-investments-in-finance/
Gi-42		Image courtesy: https://kamdora.com/2016/11/14/five-hundred-thousand-naira/
Gi-43	Individual development guide for a healthy living: A guide towards developing the right attitude for a successful business life	Image courtesy: Illustration by M.B. Bello
Gi-44	Corporate Social Responsibility	Image courtesy: https://karanjeetsingh.weebly.com/corporate-social-responsibility.html
Gi-45		Image courtesy: https://princetonacademy.in/seminar/corporate-social-responsibility/
Gi-46		Image courtesy: https://auburnpub.com/lifestyles/red-cross-the-how-to-for-nonprofit-and-business-partnerships/article_3856af3a-36b5-5480-b16f-311385f96d59.html

Image number	Description	Source
Gi-47	Business types	**Image courtesy:** Table by M.B. Bello
Gi-48	Business components for different enterprise levels	**Image courtesy:** Table by Farida Bello
Gi-49	Conclusion	**Image courtesy:** https://portal.institutohipnomind.com.br/hipnoterapia-em-sp/
Gi-50		**Image courtesy:** http://www.hsieradzki.net/WebQuest/?page_id=16

REFERENCES

Alabi J. (2016). *Sustainable Wealth Creation: an impetus for business and national growth.* Nigerian Institute of Management. North Central Zone Annual Lecture.

Angelou M. and Elliot J. M. (1989). *Conversations with Maya Angelou.* Jackson (MS): University Press of Mississippi.

Architects Registration Council of Nigeria, (2018). *Qualifications for Registration of Architects and Architectural Firms Regulation.* Available at: https://www.arconigeria.org.ng/architects-act#1

ArtzKala (2018). *Performing Arts.* Available at: https://artzkalastudio. in/performing-arts

Ashton R. (2009). *How to Start Your Own Business: for entrepreneurs.* Harlow: Pearson.

Association of Certified Chartered Accountants (2016). *Financial Accounting (ACCA F3).* Available at: https://www.youtube. com/watch?v=yf-nUGo61WE

Baker W.T. (2008). *Architectural Excellence.* Mulgrave (Vic): The Images Publishing Group. in Wikipedia (2018). *Frank Lloyd Wright.* Available at: https://en.wikipedia.org/wiki/Frank_Lloyd_Wright

CFO (2013). *Business Model Matter (for accounting, that is?)*, in Wikipedia (2018). *Business Model.* Available at: https://en.Wikipedia. org/wiki/Business_model

Courtland L. B. and William F. A. (1992). *Contemporary Advertising.* Homewood, (IL): Richard D. Irwin Inc. In Wikipedia (2018). *Advertising.* Available at: https://en.wikipedia.org/ wiki/Advertising

Davoren J. (2018). *Importance of Finance in Business.* Available at: https://yourbusiness.azcentral.com/importance-finance-business-4282.html#

Dyson J. R. (2010). *Accounting: for non-accounting students.* Harlow: Pearson.

Ewen (1976). *Captains of Consciousness.* In Wikipedia (2018). *Advertising.* Available at: https://en.wikipedia.org/wiki/ Advertising#cite_note-30

Face Book Awe Post, (2017). *Life Lesson.* in MeMe, (2018). *One of the Best Message I Have Got.* Available at: https://me.me/i/one-of-the-best-message-i-have-got-take-chances- 12787902

Financial Accounting Standards Board (2013). *FASB Exposure Draft: Recognition and measurement of Financial Assets and Financial Liabilities,* in Wikipedia (2018). *Business Model.* Available at: https:// en.Wikipedia.org/wiki/Business_model

Foreshore Waters (2018). The Riverside Waterfront Banana Island. *Daily Trust,* May 7.

Friedman S. E. (1998). *The Successful Family Business.* Chicago, (IL): Upstart Publishing Company.

Geissdoerfer M., Savaget P. and Evans S. (2017). The Cambridge Business Model Innovation Process. Procedia Manufacturing 8, 262–269, in Wikipedia, (2018). *Business Model.* Available at: https://en.wikipedia.org/wiki/Business_model

• • •

GlanzFabric (2016). *What is Fashion Design*. Available at: https://www.
quora.com/What-is-fashion-designing

Hammond B. (2010). *Interactive and Leisure Software (games and animated)*.
Available at: https://jacreativeind.wordpress.com/

Hebrero M. (2015). *Fashion Buying and Merchandising: From mass-market to
luxury retail*. In Wikipedia (2018). *Fashion design*. Available at:
https://en.wikipedia.org/wiki/Fashion_design

Howard J. R. in Encyclopaedia Britannica (2018). *Art Market*. Available
at: https://www.britannica.com/topic/art-market

Indimi M. in Business Day A7 (2018). Business in Emerging Africa:
Indimi shares lessons at Harvard. *Business Day*, May 8.

Kockritz T. (2018). *Design and Illustration*. Available at: https://
thomaskockritz.com/what-we-do/design/

Klein J. (2016). *The Value of Mentoring: push your mentee*. Available at:
https://experiencelife.com/article/the-value-of-mentoring/

Luenendonk M. (2014). *How to Set Up Accounting Department*. Available
at: https://www.cleverism.com/how-setup-accounting-
department/

Market House Books Ltd (2010). *Oxford Dictionary of Accounting*. New
York (NY): Oxford University Press.

Market House Books Ltd (2009). *Oxford Dictionary of Business and
Management*. New York (NY): Oxford University Press.

Maxwell J. C. in Rader B. (2016). *How This Entrepreneur Found Great
Mentors and Advisors*. Available at: https://www.forbes.com/
sites/bill-rader/2016/10/03/how-this-entrepreneur-found-
great-mentors-and-advisors/#7acc10f324a0

Mentor (2018). *Why Mentoring: mentoring impact.* Available at: https://www.mentoring.org/why-mentoring/mentoring-impact/

Newbigin J. in British Council, (2014). *Creative Economy.* Available at: https://creativeconomy.britishcouncil-org/guide/what-creative-economy/

Ntakhwana O. (2015). Gaebonwe Star Keeps on Rising. *Botswana Daily News,* October 26. Available at: https://allafrica.com/stories/201510270561.html

Ochi D. (2004). *Jobs and Business Opportunities in Nigeria.* Abuja (FCT): Good-thinking Consultancy & Info-Services.

Ogwu S.M. (2018). Business -1000 Entrepreneurs Storm Reality TV Heritage Audition. *Daily Trust,* August 22.

Oliver S. A. (2010). Trauma, Bodies, and Performance Art: towards an embodied ethics of seeing. <u>EBSCOhost 24,</u> 119–129. In Wikipedia (2018), *Performing Arts.* Available at: https://en.wikipedia.org/wiki/Portal:Performing_arts

Olson K. (2006). Feel Great at Any Age: the magic of mentoring. *Experience Life,* July-August. Available at: https://experiencelife.com/issues/july-august-2006/

Onmonya L. O. (2011). *Entrepreneurship and New Venture Management.* Ibadan (Oyo): Elite Press

Park S. (2006). *How to be an Entrepreneur: the six secrets of self-made success.* Harlow: Pearson.

Redstar Infowave (2017). *Digital Marketing.* Available at: www.redstarinfowave.com/mediaandadvertisement.html

Romano T. (2015). Natalie Portman, Black Swan, and the Death of the 'Triple Threat. *The Daily Beast*, Retrieved 3 April 2015 in Wikipedia (2018). *Performing Arts*. Available at: https://en.wikipedia.org/wiki/Portal:Performing_arts

Seni A. (2017). The Leadership Spark-Lab -Thriving as an Entrepreneur. *The Punch*. September 3.

Severny A. (2013). *The Movie Theatre of the Future Will Be in Your Mind*. In Wikipedia (2018). *Film*. Available at: https://en.wikipedia.org/wiki/Film

Sinha D. K. (2018). *Top 10 Types of Entrepreneurs Explained*. In Your Article Library. Available at: www.youratriclelibrary.com/entrpreneur/top-10-types-of-entrepreneurs-explained/40648

Stanton W.J. (1984). *Fundamentals of Marketing*. New York (NY): McGraw Hill. In Wikipedia, (2018) *Advertising*. Available at: https://en.wikipedia.org/wiki/Advertising

Steven D. In Wikipedia (2018). *Publishing*. Available at: https://en.wikipedia.org/wiki/publishing

The Dutch Rose (2016). *Antique*. http://thedutchrose.blogspot.com/2016/08/an-antique-is.html

WebFinance Inc. (2018). *Entrepreneurship*. Available at: http://www.businessdictionary.com/definition/entrepreneurship.html.

Wikipedia (2016). *Antique*. Available at: https://en.wikipedia.org/wiki/Antique

Wikipedia (2018). *Broadcasting*. Available at: https://en.wikipedia.org/wiki/Broadcasting

Wikipedia (2018). *Creative Industries*. Available at: https://
en.wikipedia.org.wiki/creative_industries

Wikipedia (2018). *Economy*. Available at: https://en.wikipedia.org/
wiki/Economy

Wikipedia (2018). *Performing Arts*. Available at: https://en.wikipedia.
org/wiki/Portal:Performing_arts

...ABOUT THIS BOOK...
&
LAST WORD...

...About this book...

Creativity isn't sufficient to set up an enterprise.

Therefore, a creative person needs to become an entrepreneur simply by learning how to sell his product for profit.

The Creative Industries Entrepreneur is focused on the A to Z requirements of how to be a successful entrepreneur.

The content provides the guidelines of how products and services can be taken to the marketplace with a view to sell or offer services at the appropriate price, and make a profit for savings and re-investment into possible sustainable ventures.

The book provides the most appropriate guidance for the creative persons and others to effectively unlock their entrepreneurial potentials in wealth creation.

A one-stop shop for all potential entrepreneurs.

The overall effect will have great positive impact for all and the economy.

...Last Word...

Like every building must have an architect, so also every enterprise must have an entrepreneur.

Arc. M.B. Bello, fnia

www.ingramcontent.com/pod-product-compliance
Lightning Source LLC
Chambersburg PA
CBHW042310210326
41598CB00041B/7338